Stylistics

LONDON AND NEW YORK

Stylistics

A practical coursebook

- Laura Wright
- Jonathan Hope

ROUTLEDGE

First published 1996
by Routledge
11 New Fetter Lane, London EC4P 4EE

Simultaneously published in the USA and
Canada
by Routledge
29 West 35th Street, New York, NY 10001

Text design: Barker/Hilsdon

Typeset in Sabon, Futura Book and Optima by
Solidus (Bristol) Ltd., Bristol
Printed and bound in Great Britain by
TJ Press (Padstow) Ltd, Padstow, Cornwall

*British Library Cataloguing in Publication
Data*
A catalogue record for this book is available
from the British Library

*Library of Congress Cataloguing in
Publication Data*
A catalogue record for this book has been
requested

ISBN 0–415–11381–4

In memory of J. P. Thorne (1933–1988)
whose teaching influence continues
in these pages

Contents

List of texts   x
How to use this book   xiii
Acknowledgements   xv
Permissions   xvi
List of abbreviations   xviii

1 The Noun Phrase   1

1.1 Introduction: the structure of the noun phrase   2
1.2 Premodification   5
1.3 Postmodification   12
1.4 Articles   18
1.5 Pronouns denoting the first-person singular   22
1.6 Pronouns: the first-person plural   29
1.7 Pronouns: the second person   34
1.8 Pronouns: the second person (2)   38

2 The Verb Phrase   45

2.1 Introduction: the structure of the verb phrase   46
2.2 Narrative time, story time and tense   49

2.3	Simple and compound verb phrases	55
2.4	Uses of the present tense	64
2.5	The passive	69
2.6	The imperative	72
2.7	Non-finite verb forms: '*to* + base' form (the infinitive)	77
2.8	Non-finite verb forms: '*-ing*' forms	80
2.9	Non-finite verb forms: time and tense	83

3 The Clause 89

3.1	Introduction to syntax	90
3.2	Analysing clause structure	94
3.3	The relationship between S and V	98
3.4	Relative size of syntactic elements: light X elements	102
3.5	Obligatory X elements (transitivity)	109
3.6	Expansion of X elements	112
3.7	Heavy S and X elements before the verb	116
3.8	Placement of adverbials in the clause	120
3.9	Main clauses	124
3.10	Coordination	133
3.11	Subordination and the sentence	140
3.12	Ambiguity in syntax	142
3.13	Prepositions	147
3.14	Interrogatives	156

4 Text Structure 163

4.1	Introduction to text structure: cohesion and coherence	164
4.2	Information structure: given to new	166
4.3	Ellipsis	170
4.4	Cohesion and coherence	176
4.5	Coherent models: thought	179
4.6	Coherent models: other languages	187
4.7	Coherent models: speech	195

5   Vocabulary   203

5.1   Introduction to vocabulary   204
5.2   Register: use of romance vocabulary   209
5.3   Register: use of 'long' words   213
5.4   Word-formation: bound morphemes   215
5.5   Romance   220
5.6   Semantic fields   222
5.7   Collocation   227
5.8   Synonyms   230

Index   235

Texts

(date of first publication [date of edition used])

Bambara, Toni Cade, 'Sweet Town' (1959) (5.4) and 'The Survivor' (1972) (3.2) from *Gorilla, My Love*, The Women's Press (1984).
—— *The Salt Eaters*, The Women's Press (1980) (2.9).
Beckett, Samuel, 'Molloy' (1955) from *The Beckett Trilogy: Molloy, Mallone Dies, The Unnamable*, Picador (1979) (4.4).
Bellow, Saul, *Humboldt's Gift* (1973, Penguin [1976]) (3.4).
Boehmer, Elleke, *Screens against the Sky*, Bloomsbury (1990) (3.3).
Brentford Chiswick and Isleworth Times, 3 September 1993 (5.2, 5.4).
Brookner, Anita, *A Friend from England* (1987, Grafton Books [1988]) (1.2).
—— *A Family Romance*, Jonathan Cape (1993) (3.14).
Burn, Gordon, *Alma Cogan*, Secker & Warburg (1991) (1.6, 2.5).
Carey, Peter, *The Tax Inspector*, Faber & Faber (1991) (4.1).
Chandler, Raymond, *The Big Sleep*, Hamish Hamilton (1939, Penguin [1948]) (1.8).
—— *Farewell, My Lovely* (1940, Penguin [1949]) (2.3).
—— *The Lady in the Lake*, Hamish Hamilton (1944, Penguin [1952]) (2.3).
Compton-Burnett, Ivy, *A God and His Gifts* (1963, Penguin [1983]) (4.3).
Conrad, Joseph, *Typhoon* (1903, Oxford Paperbacks [1986]) (3.13).
Deighton, Len, *Billion-Dollar Brain* (1966, Arrow [1991]) (2.3).
Dick, Philip K., *The Man in the High Castle* (1962, Penguin [1965]) (4.6).
Doyle, Roddy, *The Snapper*, Secker & Warburg (1990, Minerva [1991]) (4.4).

Faulkner, William, *The Sound and the Fury* (1931, Penguin [1964]) (3.5).
—— *Go Down, Moses*, Random House (1942) (3.11).
Fitzgerald, F. Scott, *The Great Gatsby* (1926, Penguin [1950]) (1.5, 3.13).
Fitzgerald, Zelda, 'Our Own Movie Queen' (1925) from *The Collected Writings* (1991, Abacus [1993]) (3.9).
Fleming, Ian, *From Russia with Love* (1957, Coronet [1988]) (1.3).
Green, Henry, *Living* (1929, Harvill [1991]) (3.9).
—— *Pack my Bag* (1940, Hogarth Press [1979]) (1.5).
—— *Caught* (1943, Harvill [1991]) (4.7).
—— *Concluding*, Hogarth Press (1948) (3.6).
Greene, Graham, *Brighton Rock* (1938, Penguin [1975]) (3.8).
Gibbons, Stella, *Cold Comfort Farm* (1932, Penguin [1938]) (1.7).
Hall, Adam, *The Striker Portfolio* (1969, Fontana [1975]) (2.3).
—— *The Tango Briefing* (1973, Fontana [1975]) (3.10).
Healy, Thomas, *Rolling*, Polygon (1992) (3.8).
Isherwood, Christopher, *Mr Norris Changes Trains* (1935, Meuthen [1987]) (2.8, 5.5).
James, Henry, *The Ambassadors* (1903, Penguin [1973]) (3.7).
Janowitz, Tama, 'The Slaves in New York' from *Slaves of New York* (1986, Picador [1987]) (2.1).
Johns, Captain W. E., *Biggles in Australia* (1955, Armada [1970]) (5.8).
Johnson, B. S., *Christie Malry's Own Double-Entry* (1973, Penguin [1984]) (5.3).
Joyce, James, *Ulysses* (1922, Penguin [1969]) (4.5).
Kipling, Rudyard, 'As Easy as ABC' (1912) from *A Diversity of Creatures*, Macmillan (1917) (2.2).
Laing, Kojo, *Major Gentl and the Achimota Wars*, Heinemann African Writers Series (1992) (5.7).
Lodge, David, *Nice Work*, Secker & Warburg (1988) (2.2).
McInerney, Jay, *Brightness Falls*, Bloomsbury (1992) (3.4).
Masters, John, *Bhowani Junction*, Michael Joseph (1954) (1.6).
Mathews, Harry, 'Country Cooking from Central France: Roast Boned Rolled Stuffed Shoulder of Lamb (*farce double*)' (1978) from *Miquel Barceló: Pinturas y Esculturas 1993*, Galeria Soledad Lorenzo (1994) (2.6).
Maugham, Somerset, 'My Lady's Parlour' from *On a Chinese Screen* (1922, Oxford University Press [1985]) (1.2).
Mo, Timothy, *Sour Sweet* (1982, Abacus [1983]) (3.14).
Mukherjee, Bharati, *Jasmine* (1989, Virago [1991]) (1.7).
Nabokov, Vladimir, *Lolita* (1955, Weidenfeld & Nicolson [1959]) (1.4).

Naipaul, Shiva, *A Hot Country*, Hamish Hamilton (1983) (2.7).

Naipaul, V. S., *An Area of Darkness*, Reprint Society Ltd, by arrangement with André Deutsch (1964) (3.10).

News of the World, 22 May 1994 (1.3).

Okara, Gabriel, *The Voice* (1964, Heinemann Educational [1970]) (4.6).

Orwell, George, 'Why I Write' (1947) from *Decline of the English Murder*, Penguin (1965) (1.5).

Powell, Anthony, *O, How the Wheel Becomes It!* (1983, Mandarin [1992]) (5.2).

Rhys, Jean, *Good Morning Midnight* (1939, André Deutsch [1984]) (2.4).

Richardson, Dorothy, *Pilgrimage* (1915, Virago [1979]) (4.5).

Sansom, William, *The Body*, Hogarth Press (1949) (2.7).

Selvon, Sam, *Moses Ascending*, Davis-Poynter (1975) (1.8).

Sinclair, Iain, *Downriver*, Grafton Books (1991) (5.6).

Smith, Stevie, *Novel on Yellow Paper* (1936, Virago [1980]) (4.7).

Stafford, Jean, *Boston Adventure* (1944, Hogarth Press [1986]) (1.6, 5.6).

Swift, Graham, *Shuttlecock* (1981, Penguin [1982]) (1.4).

—— *Waterland* (1983, Picador [1984]) (2.1).

Tutuola, Amos, *The Palm-Wine Drinkard*, Faber & Faber (1952) (4.6).

Wain, John, *Hurry on Down*, Secker & Warburg (1953) (4.3).

Wallington, Mark, *The Missing Postman* (1992, Warner [1993]) (4.2).

Wells, H. G., *Tono-Bungay* (1909, Pan Books [1964]) (3.12).

How to use this book

Using a wide range of twentieth-century literary prose, this book is an introduction to the techniques of stylistic analysis. The book also serves as a practical introduction to basic descriptive grammar from clause to text structure.

The book is divided into five chapters, which are subdivided into sections. Each chapter corresponds to a major area of grammar, while each section focuses on a particular feature of the area. Sections are self-contained, with a definition of the feature, a text for analysis in which use of the feature is significant, a solution, and a verdict.

Within each chapter, the higher numbered sections are more complex. Chapters 1, 2, 3, 4 are also in increasing order of complexity. However, we have placed Chapter 5 at the end, even though vocabulary is arguably the most easily grasped topic, because it is the most limited area linguistically and therefore least rewarding.

Although the chapters and sections get increasingly complex, there is no need for teachers to follow our ordering within or between blocks. One method which we have both used with success is to group three or four texts on a similar point (for example, pronouns), give them all to a class, assign one text to a group of students within the class for detailed analysis, and end the class with the groups discussing each text in turn. The teacher can begin with an introduction to the area being studied if appropriate, but we have found that it often pays to assume knowledge on the part of students: they quickly come to understand what is being looked at from the definitions, and the texts.

What the book does not do

This book does not seek to give an account or defence of stylistics as a discipline (see Michael Toolan, *The Stylistics of Fiction* (Routledge, 1990) and the journal *Language and Literature* (Longman) for this).

The book deliberately confines itself to twentieth-century fictional prose, with some non-fiction for contrast. We took this decision because we wanted to address a literary-linguistic audience, and because most of the stylistics published in this area is on poetry.

Although the book confines itself to twentieth-century fictional prose, it teaches techniques of analysis which are readily transferable to other genres of texts. Students might be encouraged to find similar features in a range of non-literary texts (or comment on their absence) as a result of working with this book.

The book does not provide whole readings of literary works. Students and teachers from a literary background may find this reductive or frustrating. We would encourage teachers to follow up the partial readings provided here with more detailed work. We have deliberately selected authors whose work deserves, and would repay, more detailed analysis using the techniques introduced here.

Acknowledgements

The authors would like to thank: Ailsa Camm; Ruth Williams; University of Hertfordshire, Department of Linguistics; University of Leeds, School of English; Julia Hall; University of London, Royal Holloway College, Department of English and Library; Loreto Todd; students of the Leeds MA course in English Language who commented on draft sections; and Norman MacLeod.

Permissions

The authors and publishers would like to thank the copyright holders for granting permission to reproduce the following:

The extract from 'Sweet Town' from *Gorilla, My Love* by Toni Cade Bambara, first published in Great Britain by The Women's Press Ltd, 1984, 34 Great Sutton Street, London EC1V 0DX, reprinted on pp. 217–18: used by permission of The Women's Press Ltd;

The extract from 'The Survivor' from *Gorilla, My Love* by Toni Cade Bambara, first published in Great Britain by The Women's Press Ltd, 1984, 34 Great Sutton Street, London EC1V 0DX, reprinted on pp. 96–7: used by permission of The Women's Press Ltd;

The extract from *The Salt Eaters* by Toni Cade Bambara, first published in Great Britain by The Women's Press Ltd, 1982, 34 Great Sutton Street, London EC1V 0DX, reprinted on pp. 85–6: used by permission of the Women's Press Ltd;

The extract from *Screens against the Sky* by Elleke Boehmer: used by permission of A. P. Watt Ltd on behalf of Elleke Boehmer;

The extract from *Alma Cogan* by Gordon Burn: used by permission of Martin Secker & Warburg;

The extract from *The Big Sleep* and *The Lady in the Lake* both by Raymond Chandler: reproduced by permission of Hamish Hamilton Ltd;

The extract from *The Snapper* by Roddy Doyle: used by permission of Martin Secker & Warburg;

The extract from 'Our Own Movie Star' from *The Collected Writings* by Zelda Fitzgerald: reprinted by permission of Harold Ober Associates, © 1991 by the Trustees of the Fitzgerald Estate;

The extract from *From Russia with Love* by Ian Fleming: used by permission of Gildrose Publications Ltd, © Gildrose Productions Ltd 1957;

The extract from *Living, Pack my Bag, Caught* and *Concluding* all by Henry Green: used by permission of Chatto & Windus and the Estate of the author;

The extract from *Rolling* by Thomas Healy: used by permission of Polygon;

The extract from *Mr Norris Changes Trains* by Christopher Isherwood: used by permission of Chatto & Windus;

The extract from *Major Gentl and the Achimota Wars* by Kojo Laing: used by permission of Heinemann;

The extract from *Nice Work* by David Lodge: used by permission of Martin Secker & Warburg;

The extract from *Jasmine* by Bharati Mukherjee, *Pilgrimage* by Dorothy Richardson and *Novel on Yellow Paper* by Stevie Smith: used by permission of Virago Press;

The extract from *Downriver* by Iain Sinclair: used by permission of HarperCollins Publishers Ltd;

The extract from *Shuttlecock* by Graham Swift: reproduced by permission of Penguin Books Ltd in the UK and by A. P. Watt Ltd in the USA on behalf of Graham Swift;

The extract from *Hurry on Down* by John Wain: used by permission of Martin Secker & Warburg.

Every effort was made to clear permission of all extracts reprinted in this book, and the publisher would be very happy to hear from copyright holders whom we have been unable to trace.

Abbreviations

AdjP	adjective phrase
aux	auxiliary
Av	adverbial
C	complement
NP	noun phrase
O	object
P	preposition
PP	prepositional phrase
S	subject
V	verb
VP	verb phrase
*	ungrammatical form

Chapter 1

The Noun Phrase

- 1.1   Introduction: the structure of the
        noun phrase   2
- 1.2   Premodification   5
- 1.3   Postmodification   12
- 1.4   Articles   18
- 1.5   Pronouns denoting the
        first-person singular   22
- 1.6   Pronouns: the first-person plural   29
- 1.7   Pronouns: the second person   34
- 1.8   Pronouns: the second person (2)   38

1.1 Introduction: the structure of the noun phrase

The simplest kinds of clause usually consist of nouns (sometimes called naming words) and verbs (doing words), for example:

Helen   saw   Bill
(noun) (verb) (noun)

However, in spoken language these positions before and after the verb are rarely occupied by just a single noun. More usually, they are filled by groups of two or more words. These groups of words are called **noun phrases** (NP) because, although they can consist of more than one word, they function in exactly the same way as a single noun:

NP(My friend)   saw   NP(Bill who comes from Leeds)

You can check that the groups of words bracketed here as noun phrases really do function as nouns by substituting *Bill* or a **pronoun** like *she*, *he* or *him*:

NP(She)   saw   NP(him)

Noun phrases consist of one **head noun,** which must always be present, and a number of further elements, all of which are optional. Noun phrases can therefore consist of only one, or very many, words. If only one word is present, it will usually be either a proper noun (a name) or a pronoun, for example:

NP(Helen) saw NP(him)
NP(She)   saw NP(Bill)

The majority of noun phrases consist of a head noun plus one or two of the optional elements. These optional elements fit into four predetermined slots in the noun phrase:

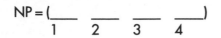

NP = (____ ____ ____ ____)
      1   2   3   4

1 = **determiner** and/or enumerator (e.g. *the, a, first, his*)
2 = pre-head modification (e.g. *red, washed, painting, steel*)
3 = head noun
4 = post-head modification (e.g. *in Leeds, which I showed you*)

for example:

NP(a   Judas Priest   T-shirt   with vents cut out)
    1   2   3   4

NP(His   size ten Doc Marten combat   boots   ____)
    1   2   3   4

NP(My   ____   friend   ____) ...
    1   2   3   4

NP(____   ____   Bill   who lives in Leeds) ...
    1   2   3   4

NP(____   ____   Benny   ____) ...
    1   2   3   4

NP(____   ____   He   ____) ...
    1   2   3   4

The optional nature of elements 1, 2 and 4 means that noun phrases have a highly variable appearance – from single words to very long passages of text, for example:

NP(____   ____   she   ____)
    1   2   3   4

NP(the   old stone   cottage   at the top of the hill which had been
    1   2   3   4
condemned but was now up for renovation and which I had always dreamed of owning) was too expensive

compare:

NP(it) was too expensive

Slots 2 and 4 in particular can be almost infinitely expanded – but note that slot 2 is usually occupied by single words (either **adjectives,** or nouns with an adjectival function), while slot 4 usually contains phrases or **clauses.** In all cases, the word in slot 3 is the most important one – it can be replaced by a pronoun, but never deleted. This is the head noun.

Stylistically, slot 4 is the most usual place to find modification of the head noun in English. This may seem strange – after all, modification in slot 2 is simpler in that it consists of single words – but it makes sense in that this allows the hearer or reader to know what the head noun is before receiving any extra information about it. Some types of text (adverts, newspaper headlines) do have modification in slot 2 more frequently as it saves space, for example:

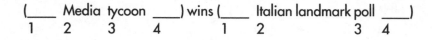

but having more than two elements in this slot quickly sounds unnatural.

Pronouns

Pronouns are a special type of noun phrase which we will be looking at in some detail. Pronouns refer to people or things, and are used to replace full nouns (hence their name).

Typically pronouns occur on their own in the noun phrase – without determiners or modification:

(he)   (she)   (I)   (it)   (they)

although **possessive pronouns** can themselves function as determiners:

(his face)
 1

(her second novel)
 1   2   3

Pronouns are structured in terms of their reference to **person** and number:

Person	Number	
	Singular	Plural
1st	I	we
2nd	you	you
3rd	he/she/it	they

and most change their form according to role within the clause:

| **subject** | I | you | he/she/it | we | you | they |
| **object** | me | you | him/her/it | us | you | them |

hence:

(I) saw (you) → (you) saw (me)

Writers can, however, achieve stylistic effects by broadening these limits of reference.

1.2 Premodification

Definition

Words which can occur in slots 1 and 2 to the left of the head are typically:

slot 1 determiners, numbers, pronouns
slot 2 adjectives, nouns

The head of the noun phrase (slot 3) is a word which is modified by modifiers to the right (slot 4) or left (slots 1 and 2) but which cannot be deleted.

One way of testing to see whether a word is a **premodifier** or not, is to pick a noun (let's take, for example, the word *ashtrays*) and put the word you suspect might be a premodifier to the left of it, for example:

EXAMPLES

> *heavy coloured glass*   ashtrays
> *six coloured Wedgwood*   ashtrays
> *her own two*   ashtrays

Exercises

Identify the premodifiers in the following:

1   listless Saturday afternoons

2   the vaguely baronial gas fire

3   dishes with gold rims

4   tiny napkins of écru linen

Comment

In (1), *listless* is an adjective; *Saturday* is a noun. We can run a test for adjectives and nouns: adjectives fit between determiners and nouns, and must be followed by a noun (e.g. *the . . . girl*); nouns fill the slot after a determiner, and do not need an adjective (e.g. *the . . .*). Here, both *listless* and *Saturday* premodify *afternoons*.

In (2), the adverb *vaguely* premodifies the adjective *baronial*, which together with *gas*, premodify *fire*.

In (3), *with gold rims* postmodifies *dishes*, and *gold* premodifies *rims*.

In (4), *of écru linen* postmodifies *napkins*. *Tiny* premodifies *napkins* and *écru* premodifies *linen*.

In the following exercise, we are interested in the lexical items which occur in premodifying position. Typically, these will be adjectives and nouns.

Identify the adjective, adverb and noun premodifiers in the noun phrase, in the following texts.

Relate your findings to the subject of the text: what is their purpose?

TEXT 1

I was not disappointed. The house – a substantial but essentially modest suburban villa – was furnished with voluptuous grandeur in approximations of various styles, predominantly those of several Louis, with late nineteenth- and early twentieth-century additions. Heavy coloured glass ashtrays of monstrous size and weight rested on inlaid marquetry tables of vaguely Pompadour associations. At dinner we drank champagne from ruby Bohemian glasses: the meat was carved at a Boulle-type sideboard. 'Regency' wallpaper of dark green and lighter green stripes was partially covered by gilt-framed landscapes of no style whatever. The dining-room seemed dark, as dining-rooms often do. In fact all the rooms seemed to repel both light and weather; they were designed to keep one's thoughts indoors, resigned and melancholy. I thought of listless Saturday afternoons, when I pictured Oscar relaxing in one of the turquoise silk-covered bergères, with foot-stools to match. I thought of Dorrie taking a nap in her shell-pink bedroom with the extravagant expanses of white shag-pile carpet. All the windows would be closed, of course, the smell of a substantial lunch still heavy on the air, slightly obscured by one of the two or three weekend cigars. Upstairs, the nap finished, and the light already beginning to fade, I imagined Dorrie switching on the vaguely baronial gas fire and pulling the satin curtains. Throwing a handful of flowery cologne over her throat and shoulders, she would change into a patterned silk dress, taking a clean handkerchief and tucking it up her sleeve. It would not be quite time for tea, but as relatives were expected she would start her preparations in the kitchen, transferring home-made cakes and biscuits on to dishes with gold rims, and laying cups and plates, interleaved with tiny napkins of écru linen, on the trolley, knives and spoons tinkling, to be wheeled in effortlessly at the right moment. For she was daintily houseproud.

TEXT 2

It was an old temple, a small one, in the city, which she had taken and was turning into a dwelling house. It had been built for a very holy monk by his admirers three hundred years before, and here in great piety, practising innumerable austerities, he had passed his declining days. For long after in memory of his virtue the faithful had come to worship, but in course of time funds had fallen very low and at last the two or three monks that remained were forced to leave. It was weather-beaten and the green tiles of the roof were overgrown with weeds. The raftered ceiling was still beautiful with its faded gold dragons on a faded red; but she did not like a dark ceiling, so she stretched a canvas across and papered it. Needing air and sunlight, she cut two large windows on one side. She very luckily had some blue curtains which were just the right size. Blue was her favourite colour: it brought out the colour of her eyes. Since the columns, great red sturdy columns, oppressed her a little she papered them with a very nice paper which did not look Chinese at all. She was lucky also with the paper with which she covered the walls. It was bought in a native shop, but really it might have come from Sandersons'; it was a very nice pink stripe and it made the place look cheerful at once. At the back was a recess in which had stood a great lacquer table and behind it an image of the Buddha in his eternal meditation. Here generations of believers had burned their tapers and prayed, some for this temporal benefit or that, some for release from the returning burden of earthly existence; and this seemed to her the very place for an American stove. She was obliged to buy her carpet in China, but she managed to get one that looked so like an Axminster that you would hardly know the difference. Of course, being hand-made, it had not quite the smoothness of the English article, but it was a very decent substitute. She was able to buy a very nice lot of furniture from a member of the Legation who was leaving the country for a post in Rome, and she got a nice bright chintz from Shanghai to make loose covers with. Fortunately she had quite a number of pictures, wedding presents and some even that she had bought herself, for she was very artistic, and these gave the room a cosy look. She needed a screen and here there was no help for it, she had to buy a Chinese one, but as she very cleverly said, you might perfectly well have a Chinese screen in England.

Solution

TEXT 1

substantial, essentially modest suburban, voluptuous, various, several, late, nineteenth, early twentieth-century, heavy coloured glass, monstrous, inlaid marquetry, vaguely Pompadour, ruby Bohemian, Boulle-type, 'Regency', dark, lighter green, gilt-framed, listless Saturday, turquoise silk-covered, shell-pink, extravagant, white shag-pile, substantial, weekend, vaguely baronial gas, satin, flowery, patterned silk, clean, home-made, gold, tiny, écru

TEXT 2

old, small, dwelling, very holy, great, innumerable, declining, long, very, green, raftered, faded gold, faded, dark, large, blue, right, favourite, great red sturdy, very nice, native, very nice pink, great lacquer, eternal, temporal, returning, earthly, very, American, English, very decent, very nice, nice bright, loose, wedding, very, cosy, Chinese, Chinese

ATTRIBUTION

Text 1 Anita Brookner, *A Friend from England*, pp. 12–13.
Text 2 Somerset Maugham, 'My Lady's Parlour' from *On a Chinese Screen*, pp. 14–16.

Verdict

TEXT 1

There are a lot of premodifiers in this passage. Some noun phrases are particularly heavy – after all, even one premodifier is optional, so to persistently find three or more is remarkable. Some are proper nouns (*Boulle, Regency, Pompadour*); and some are technical furniture terms (*shag, gilt, marquetry*). Notice how the register of some of these modifiers comes from written English and not spoken English (*écru, Bohemian*). These modifiers combine to sound like a furniture catalogue or interior-design magazine, and let the reader know that the narrator finds the house vulgar. By including so many premodifiers the description becomes pedantically accurate. *An armchair* tells the reader what a character is sitting in; that it is a *turquoise silk-covered bergère with matching foot-stool* is too much information to simply relay the act of sitting; it tells us both about the taste of the purchaser of the chair, and the opinion of the narrator upon this taste.

The narrator then goes on to tell us about the probable actions of the owners of the house, Dorrie and Oscar. Oscar relaxes and has a nap, but Dorrie prepares for guests. Note how these preparations are presented to us. The verbs are all unmodified:

> switching, pulling, throwing, would change, taking, tucking, would start transferring, laying, to be wheeled, was

But the **objects** and **complements** of these verbs are usually premodified:

> vaguely baronial gas fire, satin curtains, flowery cologne, patterned silk dress, clean handkerchief, home-made cakes and biscuits, gold rims, tiny napkins, écru linen, daintily houseproud

Now we can see that Dorrie is the architect of the interior design, and it is her taste that is detailed so precisely. What she actually does is not important to the narrator (the verbs are not modified) – but appearances are. By describing her furniture, the narrator allows us to draw moral inferences about someone who is more concerned with appearances than actions. Dedication to keeping up appearances, and the commensurate suppression of factual reality, is one of the preoccupations of much of Anita Brookner's writing. Dorrie seems harmless, indeed, possibly fussily endearing; but she is also discovered to be without moral seriousness.

TEXT 2

There are two characters in Text 2, the narrator, and the lady of the title. Ostensibly it looks as though there is only one character, the narrator, but by considering the premodifiers we can see that the opinions given are frequently those of the lady, not those of the narrator. Compare the premodifiers from the passage where the lady's parlour is being described:

> blue, right, favourite, very nice, native, very nice pink, very, American, English, very decent, very nice, nice bright, loose, wedding, very, cosy, Chinese, Chinese

with the premodifiers from the narrator's description of the temple and the activities of the monks:

> old, small, dwelling, very holy, great, innumerable, declining, long, very, green, raftered, faded gold, faded, dark, large, great red sturdy, great lacquer, eternal, temporal, returning, earthly

And consider further the adverbs from the passages describing the lady's parlour:

> very luckily, really, hardly, fortunately, very cleverly, perfectly well

The narrator is implying strongly that the lady is a snob, in that she is concerned with whereabouts her things come from (Sandersons, America and Axminster as opposed to China), and that she is making the best of what, to her, are adverse conditions. The narrator condemns her lack of education by letting us know that her pictures were given to her as wedding presents, and are there as interior décor. She has no interest in things Chinese, nor does she have any respect for the religion of the Chinese. She is oblivious to the merits of Chinese workmanship in hand-made carpets. The narrator is sneering at the lady for her adherence to

English *petit bourgeois* taste, and her refusal or inability to learn from her new surroundings.

We can also infer that the narrator has no empathy with English female conditioning at the start of the century. In a society where women were raised to be home-makers, it is not surprising that the first thing the lady does in a new environment is to turn it into a home just like her last one. Because British male and female children used to be raised very differently from each other, it would be surprising if the male writer/narrator did share the lady's attitude. For some readers, Text 2 is an amusing satire on a lower-middle-class English woman; for others, it will reveal a sexist, or unempathetic, narrator.

SUMMARY

> Both authors use the premodificatory slot in the noun phrase to describe physical artefacts, to convey the personality of characters, and also to convey the narrators' opinion of those characters.

1.3 Postmodification

Definition

There are two slots in the noun phrase for modification – 2 and 4:

    (He) (ate) (a very fresh, speckled brown egg ____)
                   1 2   3   4

    (He) (ate) (an ____ egg which was very fresh and speckled
                   1   2   3   4
    brown)

In most cases, English prefers to use slot 4 rather than slot 2 as this keeps the head noun (3) near to the front of the noun phrase.

A further possibility is for the modification to be taken out of the noun phrase and placed after the verb *to be*:

(The egg)   (was)   (fresh)

This is also more usual in English than using slot 2, especially if more than one adjective is involved. Imagine the likelihood of someone *saying* the following:

I like this really tasty beer.

or:

I like this beer. It's really tasty.

Although placing modification in slot 4, or after *to be* are more usual, slot 2 is more economical with space. For this reason, newspaper headlines often use it:

(Judo-mad   vicar)   falls for   (church   wife)
2   3   2   3

as do adverts, where the slightly unnatural placing of the adjective emphasises it at the expense of the item being sold:

Together they gallop in   (carefree   mood) and (perfect harmony).
                          2   3   2   3

Stride for stride   (the   spirited   yearling) matches   (every graceful
                     1   2   3   1   2
and effortless   movement   (of   (its   watchful   mother))).
                 3   4   1   2   3

For   (the   young   foal),   playing with mother is what life is all about!
       1   2   3
But for   (the   dappled grey thoroughbred mare), there is (a more
           1   2   3   1 2
serious vein (to this romp in (the fields)))). . .
     3   4 1   3   4 1   3

(From an advert for a porcelain figure of two horses,
News of the World, 22 May 1994)

TASK

> The following texts feature James Bond having breakfast twice – once in London, and once in Istanbul.
>
> Note the patterns of modification around the things he has for breakfast in each location.
>
> Why do they differ?

TEXT 3

Breakfast was Bond's favourite meal of the day. When he was stationed in London it was always the same. It consisted of very strong coffee, from De Bry in New Oxford Street, brewed in an American Chemex, of which he drank two large cups, black and without sugar. The single egg, in the dark blue egg cup with a gold ring round the top, was boiled for three and a third minutes.

It was a very fresh, speckled brown egg from French Marans hens owned by some friend of May in the country. (Bond disliked white eggs and, faddish as he was in many small things, it amused him to maintain that there was such a thing as the perfect boiled egg.) Then there were two thick slices of wholewheat toast, a large pat of deep yellow Jersey butter and three squat glass jars containing Tiptree 'Little Scarlet' strawberry jam; Cooper's Vintage Oxford marmalade and Norwegian Heather Honey from Fortnum's. The coffee pot and the silver on the tray were Queen Anne, and the china was Minton, of the same dark blue and gold and white as the egg cup.

TEXT 4

For ten minutes Bond stood and gazed out across the sparkling water barrier between Europe and Asia, then he turned back into the room, now bright with sunshine, and telephoned for his breakfast. His English was not understood, but his French at last got through. He turned on a cold bath and shaved patiently with cold water and hoped that the exotic breakfast he had ordered would not be a fiasco.

He was not disappointed. The yoghourt, in a blue china bowl, was deep yellow and with the consistency of thick cream. The green figs, ready peeled, were bursting with ripeness, and the Turkish coffee was jet black and with the burned taste that showed it had been freshly ground. Bond ate the delicious meal on a table drawn up beside the open window. He watched the steamers and the caiques crisscrossing the two seas spread out before him and wondered about Kerim and what fresh news there might be.

Solution

TEXT 3

(____   very strong   coffee   from De Bry . . . sugar)
1   2   3   4

(an   American   Chemex   ____)
1   2   3   4

(two   large   cups   black and without sugar)
1   2   3   4

(dark   blue egg   cup   with a gold ring round the top)
1   2   3   4

(a   very fresh speckled brown   egg   from French . . . country)
1   2   3   4

(____   French Marans   hens   owned by . . . country)
1   2   3   4

(two   thick   slices   of wholewheat toast)
1   2   3   4

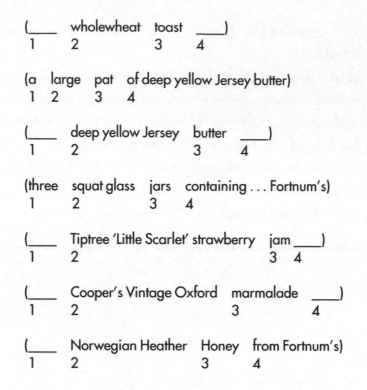

```
(___    wholewheat   toast    ___)
 1        2                3     4

(a  large   pat   of deep yellow Jersey butter)
 1    2      3     4

(___    deep yellow Jersey    butter    ___)
 1        2                     3        4

(three   squat glass   jars   containing ... Fortnum's)
 1         2            3      4

(___    Tiptree 'Little Scarlet' strawberry   jam ___)
 1        2                                    3   4

(___    Cooper's Vintage Oxford   marmalade    ___)
 1        2                         3            4

(___    Norwegian Heather   Honey   from Fortnum's)
 1        2                  3       4
```

TEXT 4

```
(The    ___    yoghourt   in a blue china bowl), was (deep yellow ...)
 1       2     3           4
(The   green   figs   ready peeled) were (bursting with ripeness)
 1      2      3      4

(the   Turkish   coffee    ___)   was   (jet black ...)
 1      2        3          4
```

ATTRIBUTION

Ian Fleming, *From Russia with Love*, pp. 80–1, 99.

Verdict

Written in the 1950s, as Britain was recovering from rationing and trying not to face up to its newly subordinate role in the world, Ian Fleming's

Bond novels have a fascination with exotic or expensive food and the superiority of British espionage. A feature of many of the stories is the breakfasts Bond has – and in these particular two meals we see Fleming handling modification very differently.

TEXT 3

Text 3 is characterised by heavy use of slot 2, and also a high frequency of trade names – which are clearly intended to carry a certain cachet. Use of slot 2 to this extent is unusual, and shifts attention away from the noun in slot 3 and on to the modification. For example: the hens are not important, but the fact that they are French is. Equally, the jam, marmalade and honey are clearly less significant than the names of their sources. In 1950s Britain, tea was the national breakfast drink, taken with plenty of milk (the top of the milk was the most coveted) and lots of white sugar. Bond, however, is ultra-sophisticated: not only does he take *coffee*, but it is *very strong*, *black* and *without sugar*. It is the modifiers that convey Bond's cosmopolitan tastes, rather than what he does or how he does it.

TEXT 4

Text 4 conforms much more closely to the norms for modification in English, making minimal use of slot 2, and more use of slot 4 and placement after *to be*. Here, the focus is on the nouns themselves: *yoghourt*, *green figs* and *freshly ground coffee* were sufficiently exotic in 1950s Britain not to need the artificial support of heavy slot-2 modification.

The premodified style of Text 3 here has passed into the modern blockbuster – and particularly the status-conscious genre known as the 'sex and shopping' novel, in which almost any item of clothing will be premodified with a designer's name, and what is in, or just about to come out of, the lingerie is no more important than the name of the shop where it was bought.

1.4   Articles

Definition

Articles qualify nouns, and appear to the immediate left in the noun phrase, before any premodifiers (slot 1). There are two articles, the **definite article** *the* and the **indefinite article** *a*. Contrast *I want the apple* (a specific, definite apple) with *I want an apple* (any, indefinite apple).

EXAMPLES

The moon was yellow.
a world apart
the reasons for *the* C9 inquiry
an assault on his son

Comment

In Standard English, *an* occurs immediately before words which begin with vowels; *a* occurs immediately before words which begin with consonants. Some other varieties of English don't follow this rule.

TASK

Identify the articles in Text 5.

Identify the part of the extract where a repetitive syntactic pattern of articles is to be found.

What is the stylistic effect of this?

Where is a similar syntactic structure to be found in Text 6, involving other parts of speech as well as articles?

What is the effect this time?

Her favourite kinds were, in this order: musicals, underworlders, westerners. In the first, real singers and dancers had unreal stage careers in an essentially grief-proof sphere of existence wherefrom death and truth were banned, and where, at the end, white-haired, dewy-eyed, technically deathless, the initially reluctant father of a show-crazy girl always finished by applauding her apotheosis on fabulous Broadway. The underworld was a world apart: there, heroic newspapermen were tortured, telephone bills ran to billions, and, in a robust atmosphere of incompetent marksmanship, villains were chased through sewers and storehouses by pathologically fearless cops (I was to give them less exercise). Finally, there was the mahogany landscape, the florid-faced, blue-eyed roughriders, the prim pretty schoolteacher arriving in Roaring Gulch, the rearing horse, the spectacular stampede, the pistol thrust through the shivered windowpane, the stupendous fist fight, the crashing mountain of dusty old-fashioned furniture, the table used as a weapon, the timely somersault, the pinned hand still groping for the dropped bowie knife, the grunt, the sweet crash of fist against chin, the kick in the belly, the flying tackle; and immediately after a plethora of pain that would have hospitalized a Hercules (I should know by now), nothing to show but the rather becoming bruise on the bronzed cheek of the warmed-up hero embracing his gorgeous frontier bride. I remember one matinee in a small airless theatre crammed with children and reeking with the hot breath of popcorn. The moon was yellow above the neckerchiefed crooner, and his finger was on his strumstring, and his foot was on a pine log, and I had innocently encircled Lo's shoulder and approached my jawbone to her temple, when two harpies behind us started muttering the queerest things — I do not know if I understood aright, but what I thought I did, made me withdraw my gentle hand, and of course the rest of the show was fog to me.

TEXT 6

Now C9 happened to be one of those cases for which Quinn himself had given me instructions but in which certain of the file items proved to have virtually no connexion at all. For example, File B in the series contained information relating to X (now deceased), a former civil servant, sacked for alcoholic incompetence and later arrested for a number of petty frauds and sexual offences, who had made allegations against a certain Home Office official, Y – allegations subsequently investigated (without Y's knowledge, either of the allegations or the investigation) and found to be false. X died of a heart attack while undergoing trial. File C in the series contained no reference to X or Y, but was a report on another Home Office official, Z, apparently unconnected, professionally or personally, with Y (or X), who had committed suicide (by stepping in front of an Underground train) shortly after the secret investigations on Y. This death was subsequently thoroughly investigated, with negative results as far as officialdom was concerned – but with great distress to the widow, who had to reveal, under pressure, intimate details about her and her husband's personal life: the mess of their marriage, his sexual incompetence, his cruelty to her, his attempting once to sleep with his nineteen-year-old daughter, an assault on his son with a garden knife, etc., etc. File D in the series was even remoter from X and Y, and File E was not on the shelves. As for the reasons for the C9 inquiry – some new evidence which had come retrospectively to light – Quinn was hanging on to this himself. When Quinn asked me about C9 I think I looked at him for signs of madness.

Solution

TEXT 5

From 'Finally, there was the mahogany landscape' to 'the warmed-up hero embracing his gorgeous frontier bride' is a list of noun phrases introduced by articles.

TEXT 6

From 'the mess of their marriage' to 'an assault on his son' is a similar list of noun phrases, introduced by articles and pronouns.

ATTRIBUTION

Text 1   Vladimir Nabokov, *Lolita*, p. 167.
Text 2   Graham Swift, *Shuttlecock*, p. 29.

Verdict

TEXT 5

The is the definite article, denoting concepts already familiar. Use of *the* indicates that not only is the narrator intimately familiar with the genre of westerns, he expects the reader to be so too. So much repetition of *the* gives a slightly ironic, faintly mocking, cynical tone, because the narrator is reducing all the westerns he has seen into one stereotypical, cliché-packed sequence. In fact, he also reveals a certain fondness for westerns, because he doesn't give this treatment to musicals and 'underworlders' (thrillers). They are summarised and dismissed much more rapidly. The narrator lingers over his description of westerns, to the extent of 21 articles introducing noun phrases, showing he's seen rather a lot of them! Far from being more sophisticated or mature than Lo in his tastes, the narrator betrays an enjoyment in watching children's matinées.

TEXT 6

The list of noun phrases in Text 6 is far shorter, but it is the same technique of quickly and briefly relating a sequence of events by means of introductory *the*, where *the* presupposes knowledge on the part of the reader. This time, the knowledge we are supposed to be already familiar with is shocking in content. Some readers will have to expand the *etc.*, *etc.*' phrases with detail gleaned only from journalism rather than experience. Again, repetition of this syntactic structure serves to give a faintly cynical tone – not this time because the narrator wishes to mock, but in order to set up a certain distance between him and the case he is describing. The narrator is not responsible for these events, he is merely a bureaucrat. The list of noun phrases reinforces the other distancing devices, such as calling people by letters, and calling files by letters too so that it is quite hard on first reading to distinguish between people and cases. All of this serves to hide the fact that people, rather than 'cases', are the topic here. The narrator is a bureaucrat in the British Civil Service, and for some readers, this impersonal treatment will render the subject-matter all the more disturbing.

1.5   Pronouns denoting the first-person singular

Definition

The first-person singular pronoun in English is *I*, which becomes *me* when placed in **object position**, and *my, mine* when denoting possession:

I am happy.	(subject)
Give it to *me*.	(object)
This is *my* book.	(possessive)
That book is *mine*.	(possessive)

However, speakers don't always wish to speak so directly about themselves. It is sometimes thought egocentric to use *I*, and at other times speakers or writers may wish to submerge their own identity in something less specific (for example, an implied group). The tactics used to do this involve a shift in person or number – into either the singular third person:

One just doesn't do that kind of thing.   (= *I* don't)

or the plural first person:

We're not at home to Mr Grumpy. (= *I'm not talking to you*)

One and *we* are ways of presenting a personal statement, yet disguising it as a more general expression. Both *one* and *we* seem to imply that the speaker is but a sub-group of a larger group of people, who also share the quality or opinion given. They are used to shift attention away from the speaker. You might find *one* to be a rather marked pronoun – marked, that is, for formality or upper-classness. Some speakers don't have *one* as part of their **idiolect** (idiolect = your own personal way of speaking) because it's not part of their dialect of English. They will use *you* as a general, impersonal pronoun in such cases. Others find it unremarkable and use it frequently, in an unmarked way.

TASK

Read the following three texts, noting the pronouns used to refer to or include the narrators.

Explain the shifts in usage within the texts.

TEXT 7

I was born a mouthbreather with a silver spoon in 1905, three years after one war and nine before another, too late for both. But not too late for the war which seems to be coming upon us now and that is a reason to put down what comes to mind before one is killed, and surely it would be asking much to pretend one had a chance to live.

That is my excuse, that we who may not have time to write anything else must do what we now can. If we have no time to chew another book over we must turn to what comes first to mind and that must be how one changed from boy to man, how one lived, things and people and one's attitude. All of these otherwise would be used in novels, material is better in that form or in any other that is not directly personal, but we I feel no longer have the time. We should be taking stock.

TEXT 8

Looking back through the last page or two, I see that I have made it appear as though my motives in writing were wholly public-spirited. I don't want to leave that as the final impression. All writers are vain, selfish and lazy, and at the very bottom of their motives there lies a mystery. Writing a book is a horrible, exhausting struggle, like a long bout of some painful illness. One would never undertake such a thing if one were not driven on by some demon whom one can neither resist nor understand. For all one knows that demon is simply the same instinct that makes a baby squall for attention. And yet it is also true that one can write nothing readable unless one constantly struggles to efface one's own personality. Good prose is like a window pane. I cannot say with certainty which of my motives are the strongest, but I know which of them deserve to be followed. And looking back through my work, I see that it is invariably where I lacked a political purpose that I wrote lifeless books and was betrayed into purple passages, sentences without meaning, decorative adjectives, and humbug generally.

TEXT 9

Reading over what I have written so far, I see I have given the impression that the events of three nights several weeks apart were all that absorbed me. On the contrary, they were merely casual events in a crowded summer, and, until much later, they absorbed me infinitely less than my personal affairs.

Most of the time I worked. In the early morning the sun threw my shadow westward as I hurried down the white chasms of lower New York to the Probity Trust. I knew the other clerks and young bond-salesmen by their first names, and lunched with them in dark, crowded restaurants on little pig sausages and mashed potatoes and coffee. I even had a short affair with a girl who lived in Jersey City and worked in the accounting department, but her brother began throwing mean looks in my direction, so when she went on her vacation in July I let it blow quietly away.

Solution

Pronouns referring to the narrator (in the order in which they ocur):

TEXT 7

I, one, one, my, we (third instance), we, one, one, one's, I

TEXT 8

I, I, my, I, one (fifth instance), one, one's, I, I, my, I, I, I

TEXT 9

I, I, I, me, me, my, I, my, I, I, I, my, I

ATTRIBUTION

Text 7 Henry Green, *Pack my Bag*, p. 5.
Text 8 George Orwell, 'Why I Write', pp. 187–8.
Text 9 F. Scott Fitzgerald, *The Great Gatsby*, pp. 62–3.

Verdict

Henry Green and George Orwell were both upper-class Englishmen and almost certainly had *one* as a variant pronoun in their idiolects. Fitzgerald, an American, may or may not have done. But whatever their personal speech patterns, when writing for the public, they could have altered their own usage, had they wanted to, for stylistic effect. Stylistically we may note that Fitzgerald is consistent, whereas Green and Orwell vary their usage. Green fights shy of *I*, whereas Orwell usually uses *I*, but breaks into a run of *one*. Why?

TEXT 7

The first extract is from the novelist Henry Green's autobiography, written at the beginning of World War II. It is the opening two paragraphs of the autobiography. The first and second instance of the pronoun *one*:

> the war which seems to be coming upon us now and that is a reason to put down what comes to mind before one is killed, and surely it would be asking much to pretend one had a chance to live

must refer to Henry Green, because he is about to engage in the act of putting down what comes to mind before he is killed, but they may also have a wider application. The reader is, to some extent, invited to identify with this exhortation and to write too.

The first two instances of *we*: 'we who may not have time to write anything else must do what we now can', also seem to have a fairly wide comprehension, encompassing not only Henry Green, but also all those people who write. Of the second group of *we*'s, the first *we* excludes all people who are not authors, and the second includes Henry Green only. 'If we have no time to chew another book over' implies that the referent(s) has/have already written at least one book. With regard to the second *we* ('we must turn to what comes first to mind'), only the speaker can know what comes first to mind. Coming first to mind is not an activity that a group of people can share. Therefore, the next pronoun, *one*, must also refer to Green: 'how one changed from boy to man'. All the following instances of *one* also refer to 'what comes first to mind', and hence refer to Henry Green only. The next two instances of *we* are thrown into contradistinction by the interpolation 'I feel', and have a global referent, that is, all who read this book at this date.

Why does Green shift from *I* to *we* to *one*, when *I* would do throughout? The opening two paragraphs serve as an apology or explanation for why he is writing his autobiography at all. Writing an autobiography runs the risk of seeming arrogant. Why pour out your intimate affairs to strangers? In an attempt to deflect such criticism, Green claims that autobiography-writing is a duty to those living on the brink of war. Similarly, by sheltering behind *one* and *we*, he evades the accusation of egotism. It is a form of modesty – though to some extent, a false one. For although fear of death is given as an excuse for writing about himself instead of inventing a story, write about himself, at great length, is what he then does.

TEXT 8

Text 8 is the last paragraph of Orwell's essay, 'Why I Write'. The *one* pronouns:

> One would never undertake such a thing if one were not driven on by some demon whom one can neither resist nor understand. For all one knows that demon is simply the same instinct that makes a baby squall for attention. And yet it is also true that one can write nothing readable unless one constantly struggles to efface one's own personality.

come in between the opening and closing *I* forms, and can be seen to be triggered by the phrase 'All writers', where Orwell suddenly shifts from the specific ('Why I write') to the general (why *all* writers write).

The middle section of this paragraph is in fact full of highly contentious subjective opinion – but it is opinion presented as generalised fact via the use of the pronoun *one* rather than *I*. Note the sentence 'And yet it is also true that one can write nothing readable unless one constantly struggles to efface one's personality.' This is presented as being a necessary condition for all writers – yet much writing deliberately investigates and lays bare the writer's personality. Even if this is true of Orwell (which is highly debatable) it is not true for all writers and all writing. The use of *one* is something of a rhetorical sleight of hand – Orwell presents personal polemic as general consensus in much the same way as he uses *to be* to form statements of apparently unqualified truthfulness which are actually unfounded assertions:

> All writers *are* vain . . .
> Writing a book *is* a horrible, exhausting struggle . . .
> it *is* also true that . . .

Ironically, Orwell then goes on to state that 'Good prose is like a window pane.' This simile seems to convey the sense that good prose is not indirect or general, but clear and specific. None the less Orwell himself disguises his own opinion as generic fact. Why should he do this? We have stated that use of *one* or *we* to mean *I* shifts attention away from the speaker. It may be that Orwell is demonstrating his desire to efface his personality in this way. But it may also be that he is not entirely open at this point. Compare Text 9, a story related by a fictional narrator.

TEXT 9

> Reading over what I have written so far, I see I have given the impression that the events of three nights several weeks apart were all that absorbed me. On the contrary, they were merely casual events in a crowded summer...

The author, F. Scott Fitzgerald, is telling a story through a fictional narrator called Nick Carraway. Compare the structure of the opening sentence of Text 9 with the opening sentence of Text 8.

> Looking back through the last page or two, I see that I have made it appear as though my motives in writing were wholly public-spirited. I don't want to leave that as the final impression. All writers are vain, selfish and lazy...

These texts are very similar in structure:

> 8 Reading over what I have written so far
> 9 Looking back through the last page or two
>
> 8 I see I have
> 9 I see that I have
>
> 8 given the impression that
> 9 made it appear as though
>
> 8 the events of three nights several weeks apart were all that absorbed me
> 9 my motives in writing were wholly public-spirited
>
> 8 On the contrary, they were merely casual events in a crowded summer
> 9 I don't want to leave that as the final impression. All writers are vain, selfish and lazy

In addition to this structural similarity, both texts involve a degree of self-consciousness about the writing process. Why then does Orwell shift in pronoun use, while Fitzgerald's use remains stable? We have suggested that Orwell's shifts are for rhetorical effect – and may involve a degree of duplicity in that they allow him to hide his personality behind a generalised, impersonal front. As far as Fitzgerald is concerned, however, his narrator is already a front – a persona who may or may not represent the author's point of view, and whose story can be regarded as not being Fitzgerald's own.

SUMMARY

Whatever their own personal usage, all writers can, if they choose, vary their pronoun usage when referring to the first-person singular. It will have a stylistic effect if they do: usually, a distancing one. Here, it seems to us that Green is apologetic because fear of death is prompting him to write his autobiography, and his use of *one* and *we* helps him to both convey and hide this fact. Orwell's shift into *one* occurs at a point when he is ostensibly being frank and admitting to personality defects. It causes us to distrust his message.

1.6   Pronouns: the first-person plural

Definition

We is the pronoun form referring to the speaker plus others. There can be ambiguity in the interpretation of the first-person plural pronoun. Does the *we* include the person spoken to, or just the speaker and his/her group?

> We don't take to your sort round here.   (exclusive)
> Will we meet for lunch at one then?   (inclusive)

Furthermore, *we* can be used in a way which implies that it is actually a singular form, as when doctors address their patients:

And how are we today then?

TASK

> Read the following texts, noting the usages of *we* – are they inclusive/
> exclusive or singular/plural?

TEXT 10 ▄▄

I said I supposed I would not drink beer again and the prospect saddened me. My teacher then laid a damp hand on mine and said, 'There, there, it's hard, poor child, but we mustn't cry,' and though she was not, of course, referring to the beer, I decided that my life would be unendurable without it. 'We' had had until now no urge to cry, but her words, so mushy and stale and yet so tender and personal, started up a torrent of tears, and each time my inquisitive tongue received a drop, I was reminded, bitterly, of the way my father had put salt in his beer. I suffered her to lay her moist fingers on my head and arms and to come quite close to me in an embrace in which all the unhealthy odors she dispensed rose and eddied about me at the slightest movement on the part of either one of us.

'We must be *brave* and not be a burden to Mother who is bringing a baby into the world just for *us*,' and then, to distract me, she said, in a fun-loving way, 'I'll tell you what: I'll bet you a dollar to a doughnut it's a boy.'

TEXT 11

Alma Cogan, yeh?

Starting from the feet we had: suede cowboy boots, pressed jeans, Navajo buckle, turquoise Navajo ring, plain T-shirt, linen jacket, inflamed nostrils, pupils like coal-holes, tumbling long blond androgynous hair. A portable phone jammed into his back pocket had the incidental effect of drawing the denim tighter at the front and showcasing his (bulked out?) thing (many hours in front of the mirror evidenced here). 'Knockout. Well-pleased. Would it be cool to lay my rap on you since you're like here?'

She said, 'We think God fixed everything in India so it can't alter. The English despise us but need us. We despise the Indians, but we need them. So it's all been fixed – the English say where the trains are to go to, we take them there, and the Indians pay for them and travel in them.'

Now she was getting excited, and her eyes sparkled, and she didn't talk la-di-da, she talked the way we do. She said, 'I've been four years among only Englishmen and Indians. Do you realize that they hardly know there *is* such a thing as an Anglo-Indian community? Once I heard an old English colonel talking to an Indian – he was a young fellow, a financial adviser. The colonel said, "What are you going to do about the Anglo-Indians when we leave?" "We're not going to do anything, Colonel," the Indian said. "Their fate is in their own hands. They've just got to look around and see where they are and who they are – after you've gone."'

Solution

TEXT 10

Second-person singular (*you*): 'you mustn't cry'

TEXT 11

First-person singular (*I*) as well as first-person plural (*everybody*): 'everybody had', 'I had'

TEXT 12

First-person plural (*we*) with varying exclusions or inclusions depending on the speaker as detailed below

ATTRIBUTION

Text 10   Jean Stafford, *Boston Adventure*, p. 73.
Text 11   Gordon Burn, *Alma Cogan*, pp. 114–15.
Text 12   John Masters, *Bhowani Junction*, p. 24.

Verdict

The first-person plural pronoun need not necessarily be plural in referent. Further, it may or may not include the speaker and/or reader: it can be exclusive in referent as well as inclusive.

TEXT 10

In Text 10 the teacher is using the kind of language adults use to children when she says to the child 'we mustn't cry' and 'we must be brave'. The first-person plural pronoun actually has a singular referent, the child. The child is, in fact, rather too old to be addressed in this way and so the teacher's clumsy attempts at comforting are perceived as patronising rather than pacifying.

TEXT 11

Text 11 has only one instance of *we*, 'Starting from the feet we had:', yet it sets the ironical, mocking tone of the passage. The fictionalised narrator is Alma Cogan, a British pop singer from the 1950s, and she is being approached by a man who, by his stereotyped appearance, looks as if he works, or would like to work, in the record business. This use of *we* is also singular in referent, in that the narrator is speaking only for herself; yet it is also global and impersonal (compare the paraphrases: *starting from the feet one had*, or *starting from the feet there was*, or, losing the mockery, *starting from the feet he wore*). This use of *we* serves to divide the approaching PR man from the rest of humanity, thereby aligning Alma Cogan with the reader. The effect is inclusive, uniting narrator and reader in a common reaction to the approach of the newcomer.

TEXT 12

This text is taken from a novel about the status of people of mixed ancestry in India. It focuses, by contrast, on the exclusive properties of *we*:

1   we think God fixed everything in India

(we Anglo-Indians)

2   we despise the Indians, but we need them

(we Anglo-Indians)

3   we take them there

(we Anglo-Indians)

4   she talked the way we do

(we Anglo-Indians?)

5   when we leave

(we Englishmen)

6   we're not going to do anything

(we Indians)

Each of the three racial groups uses *we* to exclude the other two groups. Inherent in inclusion with one group is exclusion from the others. The Indian shows by his emphasis on the word *we* ('*We*'re not going to do anything') that the cohesive group of residents in India identified by the English colonel doesn't in fact exist. Rather, the Indians perceive themselves as separate from the Anglo-Indian community, and vice versa. Neither the English nor the Indians wish to have any responsibility for the Anglo-Indians. This text is about identity; in particular, about how difficult it is for the Anglo-Indians to have any self-identity in a society where social hierarchy depends on racial background. The pronoun *we* can take on hostile overtones when used to distinguish one group of speakers from another in this way.

SUMMARY

> *We* can be put to several uses, with effect. It may include the reader, or convey lack of affiliation, as well as affiliation.

1.7   Pronouns: the second person

Definition

In strict grammatical terms, *you* is the pronoun used to address one person (singular) or more than one (plural). However, just as *one* can be used generally, and *we* can be used in the singular, the referent of *you* in actual usage can be surprising.

TASK 1

> Look at the *you* forms in the following text – do they all have the same reference?

TEXT 13

'Little Ricky Ricardo,' she said. She squeaked her nails up and down the spine of the book. I could tell she was hurting. 'It can't mean much to you.'

'You'll be okay.'

'So I waited too long,' she said. 'I wrote poems. I was going to be the next Adrienne Rich. I mean, it isn't the end of the world or anything.'

She got me there, too.

'You have nice hips,' she said. But she gave the 'you' a generic sweep. You teeming millions with wide hips breeding like roaches on wide-hipped continents. 'Wide. Nature meant you to carry babies.'

'Thank you,' I said. What else could I have said?

'You're pregnant, aren't you?' I didn't deny it. 'It was easy, wasn't it? You didn't wait, you're lucky.'

The truth is, I am young enough to bear children into the next century. But. I feel old, very old, millennia old, a bug-eyed viewer of beginnings and ends. In the old Hindu books they say that in the eye of the creator, mountains rise and fall like waves on the ocean.

TASK 2

What person forms does this text use to refer to the old woman?
Why do the forms pattern as they do?

TEXT 14

The weakening winds of spring fawned against the old house. The old woman's thoughts cowered in the hot room where she sat in solitude . . . She would not see her niece . . . Keep her away . . .

Make some excuse. Shut her out. She had been here a month and you had not seen her. She thought it strange, did she? She dropped hints that she would like to see you. You did not want to see her. You felt . . . you felt. . . some strange emotion at the thought of her. You would not see her. Your thoughts wound slowly round the room like beasts rubbing against the drowsy walls. And outside the walls the winds rubbed like drowsy beasts. Half-way between the inside and the outside walls, winds and thoughts were both drowsy. How enervating was the warm wind of the coming spring . . .

When you were very small – so small that the lightest puff of breeze blew your little crinoline skirt over your head – you had seen something nasty in the woodshed.

You'd never forgotten it.

You'd never spoken of it to Mamma – you could smell, even to this day, the fresh betel-nut with which her shoes were always cleaned – but you'd remembered all your life.

That was what had made you . . . different. That – what you had seen in the tool-shed – had made your marriage a prolonged nightmare to you.

Somehow you had never bothered about what it had been like for your husband . . .

That was why you had brought your children into the world with loathing. Even now, when you were seventy-nine, you could never see a bicycle go past your bedroom window without a sick plunge at the apex of your stomach . . . in the bicycle shed you'd seen it, something nasty, when you were very small.

That was why you stayed in this room. You had been here for twenty years, ever since Judith had married and her husband had come to live at the farm. You had run away from the huge, terrifying world outside these four walls against which your thoughts rubbed themselves like drowsy yaks. Yes, that was what they were like. Yaks. Exactly like yaks.

Solution

TEXT 13

you singular × 2; *you* generic × 4; *you* singular × 5

TEXT 14

In the first paragraph the old woman is referred to in the third person. Subsequently she is referred to in the second-person singular.

ATTRIBUTION

Text 13   Bharati Mukherjee, *Jasmine*, pp. 34–5.
Text 14   Stella Gibbons, *Cold Comfort Farm*, pp. 113–14.

Verdict

TEXT 13

Text 13 is explicit about the ambiguity inherent in *you* – which can be either singular or plural, specific or general. In fact, many dialects of English avoid this ambiguity by distinguishing between plural and singular formally, for example:

you singular   *youse* plural
you singular   *you all* plural

TEXT 14

Text 14 illustrates a more complex use of *you*. Here, the shift from third to second person (*the old woman – she – you*) comes as the narrative enters the old woman's thoughts and represents them directly ('Make some excuse ... shut her out'). It is possible therefore to see this second-person form as standing for a first-person *I*. The technique allows the author to be 'inside' the character's head in a vivid and direct way (more directly than third person would allow) while retaining a sense of distance which is vital to the humour and irony the passage creates – as the woman's thoughts ramble from woodshed to toolshed to bikeshed to drowsy yaks.

1.8 Pronouns: the second person (2)

Definition

You can refer to one specific person, addressed by the speaker, or several specific persons, addressed by the speaker.

You can also refer to any or all people in an unspecific way, for example:

> You've got to laugh, or else you'd cry.

Speakers can use *you* to refer to themselves, in an impersonal way, for example:

> I didn't think about the consequences, because if you do that, you'd never get anywhere.

In this kind of usage, the apparent switch of person merely disguises a continuity of referent. It is an attempt to objectify what is a subjective argument since such usages present a personal opinion as if it was a general one, shared by all people. These impersonal uses of pronouns can be a way of avoiding appearing self-centred, or they can attempt to deceive – to pass something contentious off as inevitable, or generally agreed upon.

Authors may use this ambiguity of referent for stylistic effect – is the *you* a singular usage, referring to a character in the novel; or is it a plural *you*, including the reader?

EXAMPLES

> *Singular, specific person*
> Paul, have you done your homework?

> *Plural, specific person*
> You two, come here.

> *General, direct address*
> You want to be with the Prudential.

General, unspecific address
You can't beat a nice cup of tea.

Identify the *you* pronouns in Text 15.
    What kinds of *you* pronouns are they?
    Contrast this type of reference with that of the other pronouns
in the text – *I/me/my*, *he/his*, *they*, *her*.
    Why does the passage use *you* in the way it does?

TEXT 15

I went quickly away from her down the room and out and down the tiled staircase to the front hall. I didn't see anybody when I left. I found my hat alone this time. Outside the bright gardens had a haunted look, as though small wild eyes were watching me from behind the bushes, as though the sunshine itself had a mysterious something in its light. I got into my car and drove off down the hill.

What did it matter where you lay once you were dead? In a dirty sump or in a marble tower on top of a high hill? You were dead, you were sleeping the big sleep, you were not bothered by things like that. Oil and water were the same as wind and air to you. You just slept the big sleep, not caring about the nastiness of how you died or where you fell. Me, I was part of the nastiness now. Far more a part of it than Rusty Regan was. But the old man didn't have to be. He could lie quiet in his canopied bed, with his bloodless hands folded on the sheet, waiting. His heart was a brief, uncertain murmur. His thoughts were as grey as ashes. And in a little while he too, like Rusty Regan, would be sleeping the big sleep.

On the way downtown I stopped at a bar and had a couple of double Scotches. They didn't do me any good. All they did was make me think of Silver-Wig, and I never saw her again.

Solution

The *you* forms in this text, all of them concentrated in the first few lines of the second paragraph, refer to everyone, including the reader and the narrator. They could be replaced (though with a change in stylistic effect) by the third-person singular pronoun *one*.

The referents of the other pronouns are much more specific: *I/me/my* to the narrator (although he is not named here, this is Philip Marlowe, the private detective played by Humphrey Bogart in many films); *he/his* to the old man; *they* to the drinks; *her* to Silver-Wig. Note too how the *I*, *you* and *he* pronouns are kept separate in the first two paragraphs, apart from the pivotal *Me, I*, which marks the shift from *you* to *he*.

ATTRIBUTION

Raymond Chandler, *The Big Sleep*, p. 220.

Verdict

This passage is the closing scene of Raymond Chandler's novel *The Big Sleep*. Chandler wrote detective fiction, but he is also widely recognised as an exceptional stylist, someone who could combine the narrative energy demanded by the thriller form with the interest in character and moral seriousness of the 'literary' novel. This passage illustrates how he manages to deal with 'big issues' – death and guilt – without sounding pretentious. Note the simple syntactic style of **coordination**, or single-clause sentences, but most of all note how the use of generic *you* allows Chandler to introduce universal issues without sententiousness. The passage proceeds syntactically from first-person pronoun clustering, to second-person pronoun clustering, to third-person pronoun clustering. All treat the subject of death, the great social leveller; and on this moral note the novel closes.

In each novel he appears in, Marlowe participates in scenes of high emotional content. Yet his wit is always dry, his speech terse. How then is he to reflect on matters of such universal magnitude as death, without resorting to purple prose or subordinate clauses? Chandler's solution here is to embrace all persons, by means of pronoun development. Were Marlowe to address mankind, or to use such items of vocabulary as *humanity* or even *man*, his reflections would appear sententious. This is partly because *man* is so general that it is hard to identify with. Compare the stylistic effect of 'What does it matter where man lies once he is dead?' with the original. Although the *you* in this sentence has a general, third-person referent, it also includes 'you, the reader', and hence strikes the personal note. By contrasting the second person with the first person, Marlowe is given a certain bitter, dismissive edge.

The use of *you*, with its connotations of direct address as well as general address, allows Chandler to deal with these issues in a non-abstract way – making them real to the reader. The lack of distance implied by *you* (rather than *one*) makes the musings on mortality something more than just literary padding. The rigid separation of pronouns, and simple syntax, mean that the passage relies on the seriousness of its topics for effect, not deliberately inflated language.

TASK

Chandler's *you* was consistently generic, but it is possible for writers to use generic *you* in a less clear-cut way.

What are the precise ranges of reference of *you* in the following?

(You will notice dialect features in this text – they are listed in the Verdict, but do not affect the usage of *you*.)

TEXT 16

I was admiring a bevy of them as they come trouncing in the market in Shepherd's Bush one morning. They make for one of those shops what does sell everything for the head except brains. Iron comb to straighten your hair, pomades and lotions to make it shine, and of course, wigs. Wigs is in now.

All kinds of Afro hair styles on display in the shop window, mixed up with some blondy, long-haired ones for those who have aspirations to be fair.

The girls stand up by the window looking in like professional head hunters, then they went in and start to try on wigs. I don't know if you have seen them women in C & A or Woolworths trying on hats, how they turn and twist and do Yoga exercises in an attempt to change their physiognomies to suit the hat they fancy. Also, the fashion being fairly new, they had to experiment and pit their wits against this latest female accoutrement.

The trouble with a wig, as I see it, is not that you trying on a new suit or a pair of shoes. It is actually going to be a part of you, like a new hand or nose or something. A time will doubtless come when you could buy a complete new face, or fit a different upper lip, or purchase a pair of new ears over the counter and put them on right away. But the greatest invention will be when you can walk in black as midnight and emerge as pure and white as the driven snow.

Solution

Referents of *you*: the reader (with curly hair), the reader, anyone, the reader, everybody, everybody (in particular, black people).

ATTRIBUTION

Sam Selvon, *Moses Ascending*, p. 22.

Verdict

Sam Selvon, a Trinidadian, wrote in a mix of Trinidadian English and London English. This is not the point we want to dwell on here (in this section we're concerned with the purposes authors put pronouns to); but here's a rapid checklist of Trinidadian English features found in the text:

- auxiliary *be* may be absent:

  > not that you trying on a new suit

- the simple present tense is used, where Standard English would use either the past tense, or a compound tense:

  > they make for one of those shops
  > as they come trouncing in

- the subject and verb don't have to agree in number:

  > wigs is in now

- the verb *do* marks a habitual aspect:

  > one of those shops what does sell everything for the head

- singular rather than plural nouns are used for generic purposes:

  > iron comb to straighten your hair

These are all features of Trinidadian English and hence are a feature of any writer who chooses to write in Trinidadian English, not just Sam Selvon.

Text 2 shows a subtle usage of *you*, with shifting referents not made explicit:

1   iron comb to straighten your hair

2   I don't know if you have seen them women in C & A or Woolworths.

3   The trouble with a wig, as I see it, is not that you trying on a new suit.

4   It is actually going to be a part of you.

5   A time will doubtless come when you could buy a complete new face.

6   But the greatest invention will be when you can walk in black as midnight.

(1) refers to all who read this text, but only those readers with curly hair will actually be able to identify with it. This will include black readers, but plenty of other readers as well. So it's a second-person plural usage. (2) refers to all who read this text, not only those who've seen women trying on hats in C & A or Woolworths, but those of us who have are invited to identify especially with this usage. Again, a plural referent. (3) refers to all readers who buy suits or shoes, so it is plural. (4) is a singular usage as each reader has only one body. (Compare the paraphrase: *it is actually going to be a part of your body*). In (5), *you* could be substituted by *one*, so it is a third-person singular usage. (6) refers to all readers, so is a plural usage, but it assumes that the reader is black.

In this passage the instances of *you* start off as general, referring to all readers, and then become specific, referring to you yourself (4). (5) is generic, yet still includes a personal identification on the part of the reader, so that by the time the reader reaches (6), the reader identifies with the referent, whether black or not.

•   •   •

Chapter 2

The Verb Phrase

- 2.1 Introduction: the structure of the verb phrase 46
- 2.2 Narrative time, story time and tense 49
- 2.3 Simple and compound verb phrases 55
- 2.4 Uses of the present tense 64
- 2.5 The passive 69
- 2.6 The imperative 72
- 2.7 Non-finite verb forms: '*to* + base' form (the infinitive) 77
- 2.8 Non-finite verb forms: '*–ing*' forms 80
- 2.9 Non-finite verb forms: time and tense 83

2.1 Introduction: the structure of the verb phrase

Just as noun phrases are built up around a head noun, so verb phrases (VP) consist of an obligatory **main verb** to which other, **auxiliary** (aux), verbs may be added, as well as **negative particles** and adverbs. For example:

> He VP(*presses*) the snooze button

> She VP(*may see*) me
> *may* = auxiliary

> He VP(*does not greatly care*) for the dark purplish bathroom suite
> *does* = aux, *not* = negative, *greatly* = adverb

> I VP(*'ve always wanted*) an en suite bathroom
> *'ve* = aux, *always* = adverb

If, as in all the examples above, the first verb in the verb phrase has **tense**, then the verb phrase is said to be **finite**. You can show that a verb phrase has tense by changing it:

> He VP(*presses*) the snooze button →
> He VP(*pressed*) the snooze button

> He VP(*does not greatly care*) for the dark purplish bathroom suite →
> He VP(*will not greatly care*) for the dark purplish bathroom suite

In addition to being marked for tense, finite verbs agree in person and number with the subject noun phrase. Again this can be demonstrated by changing the subjects:

> He VP(*presses*) the snooze button →
> I VP(*press*) the snooze button

> He VP(*does not greatly care*) for the dark purplish bathroom suite →
> They VP(*do not greatly care*) for the dark purplish bathroom suite

He VP(*'s always wanted*) an en suite bathroom →
They VP(*'ve always wanted*) an en suite bathroom

Not all verb phrases have tense or person/number agreement however. In the following examples, each sentence has two verb phrases, but only one can be changed in the ways shown above:

The only escape VP(*was*) for him VP(*to press*) the snooze button →
The only escape VP(*is*) for him VP(*to press*) the snooze button   (Tense)
The only escapes VP(*are*) for them VP(*to press*) the snooze button
(Number)

VP(*Not caring greatly*) for the bathroom suite, he VP(*kept*) out of the bathroom →
VP(*Not caring greatly*) for the bathroom suite, he VP(*keeps*) out of the bathroom   (Tense)
VP(*Not caring greatly*) for the bathroom suite, they VP(*keep*) out of the bathroom   (Number)

VP(*Wanted*) by no one, the room with the en suite bathroom VP(*was*) empty →
VP(*Wanted*) by no one, the room with the en suite bathroom VP(*is*) empty   (Tense)
VP(*Wanted*) by no one, the rooms with the en suite bathroom VP(*are*) empty   (Number)

Despite appearances, *caring* and *wanted* are not present and past tense here – they can appear with another verb in any tense at all (e.g. *Wanted by no one, the room* is/was/will be *empty*). Nor is it possible to inflect them for number. Verb phrases like this are **non-finite**.

Of the two types of verb phrase, finite ones are more common, and can stand alone, whereas non-finite verb phrases usually have to be accompanied by a finite verb phrase, as the examples show.

Finite verb phrases

As far as stylistic analysis is concerned, the most significant features of finite verb phrases are tense and voice.

We normally assume that 'tense' refers to time, and that 'present tense' and 'past tense' verbs refer to events in the present or past respectively. It is true that simple past tense forms usually do refer to events in the past, for example:

I VP(*walked*) home
He VP(*went*) to work with a song in his heart

but it is not the case that simple present tense is used exclusively, or even frequently, for events in the present. Normally the simple present is used for habitual events (which happen in the past, present and future!):

In the morning I clean up some, I walk his Dalmatian, Andrew, then I come back and cook Stash two poached eggs, raisin tea biscuits, coffee with three spoons sugar. Usually around this time of day, the doorman buzzes on the intercom and I have to go down to pick up a package, or run to the store for more cigarettes, whatever. Then Stash goes off to work.

(Tama Janowitz, 'The Slaves in New York',
from *Slaves of New York*, p. 8)

Occasionally the simple present is used to narrate events which took place in the past, as a way of making them seem more immediate (the following comes from a section of a novel in which the narrator recalls his childhood):

And Dick, while I watch, clambers onto his bed and, reaching up to the precariously perched glass and mahogany case, containing the stuffed and mounted carcase of a twenty-one-pound pike, caught on Armistice Day by John Badcock, puts his hand through one of its side panels.

(Graham Swift, *Waterland*, p. 273)

If an event is actually happening in the present, we usually put it into a construction using *be* + verb + *-ing*:

I'*m talking* to you on Sara's phone.

The normal tense for narratives in English is the simple past, but writers can vary this into the present, or into compound tenses (using the auxiliary verbs *will* for future or *to have* and *to be* for past compounds). Most texts have a mixture of simple and compound tenses.

In most clauses, the noun phrase in subject position (S) also refers to the **agent** or performer of the action, for example (V = verb, O = object):

> S(She)   V(read)   O(the newspaper)

This is an **active** clause (the subject, *she*, is doing the verb).

It is possible to rewrite such a clause in a way that reverses the positions of the subject and object:

> S(The newspaper)   V(was read)   O(by her)

This is a **passive** clause (the subject, *the newspaper*, is having the verb done to it).

It is even possible to remove the agent completely:

> S(The newspaper)   V(was read)

Stylistically, this downplays, or obscures, the agent of a deed, and focuses attention on the thing which has something done to it.

2.2 Narrative time, story time and tense

Definition

There are only two morphological tenses in English – simple past and simple present:

> *Present* I walk   She sings
> *Past*   I walked   She sang

(**Morphological** here means that the change in tense is signalled by a change in the spelling of the verb.)

All of the other tenses are formed by adding **auxiliary verbs** to the verb phrase:

> I *will* see.
> I *had* seen.
> I *had been* seeing.

Writers can use these various compound tenses to create layers of time which exist in relation to each other. For example, the normal tense used in fictional narrative is the simple past:

> I saw.

but this use of the past automatically implies a *now* of narration – the time at which the narrator speaks, or writes. So immediately in most texts we have an implied *now* of narration and a contrasted *then* of the narrated events:

> As I write this I remember how I saw . . .
> now → then

It is relatively rare for writers to make this implied *now* of narration explicit, as it distances their work from the reader. More usually, the *then* of the narrative becomes an implicit present – as readers we read past narratives as if they were happening. The compound tense system can aid this by allowing writers to shift back from the *then* of narrative to a previous *then*:

> He realised he had been hurt.
> then → before then

Potentially, any text has a complex time structure: a time of narrating, a time of narrative, and times before and after this.

Identify the times of narrating, narrative, and internal time
relationships in the following texts.
   Does tense correlate with time in English?

TEXT 1

Instantly, by some perverse chemistry of his body or nervous system, he feels
tired and drowsy, reluctant to leave the warm bed. He presses the snooze
button on the clock with a practised finger and falls effortlessly asleep. Five
minutes later, the alarm wakes him again, cheeping insistently like a
mechanical bird. Vic sighs, hits the Off button on the clock, switches on his
bedside lamp (its dimmer control turned low for Marjorie's sake) gets out of
bed and paddles through the deep pile of the bedroom carpet to the *en suite*
bathroom, making sure the connecting door is closed before he turns on the
light inside. Vic pees, a task requiring considerable care and accuracy since
the toilet bowl is lowslung and tapered in shape. He does not greatly care for
the dark purplish bathroom suite ('Damson', the estate agent's brochure had
called the shade) but it had been one of the things that attracted Marjorie
when they bought the house two years ago – the bathroom, with its kidney-
shaped handbasin and goldplated taps and sunken bath and streamlined loo
and bidet. And, above all, the fact that it was '*en suite*'. I've always wanted
an *en suite* bathroom, she would say to visitors, to her friends on the phone,
to, he wouldn't be surprised, tradesmen on the doorstep or strangers she
accosted in the street. You would think '*en suite*' was the most beautiful phrase
in any language, the lengths Marjorie went to introduce it into her
conversation. If they made a perfume called *En Suite*, she would wear it. Vic
shakes the last drops from his penis, taking care not to sprinkle the shaggy
pink nylon fitted carpet, and flushes the toilet. The house has four toilets, a
cause of concern to Vic's father. FOUR toilets? he said, when first shown over

the house. Did I count right? What's the matter, Dad? Vic teased. Afraid the water table will go down if we flush them all at once? No, but what if they start metering water, eh? Then you'll be in trouble. Vic tried to argue that it didn't make any difference how many toilets you had, it was the number of times you flushed them that mattered, but his father was convinced that having so many toilets was an incitement to unnecessary peeing, therefore to excessive flushing. He could be right, at that. At Gran's house, a back-to-back in Easton with an outside toilet, you didn't go unless you really had to, especially in the winter. Their own house in those days, a step up the social ladder from Gran's, had its own indoor toilet, a dark narrow room off the half-landing that always niffed a bit, however much Sanilav and Dettol his mother poured into the bowl. He remembered vividly that yellowish ceramic bowl with the trademark 'Challenger', the big varnished wooden seat that was always pleasantly warm to the bum, and a long chain dangling from the high cistern with a sponge-rubber ball, slightly perished, on the end of it. He used to practise heading, flicking the ball from wall to wall, as he sat there, a constipated schoolboy. His mother complained of the marks on the distemper. Now he is the proud owner of four toilets – damson, avocado, sunflower and white, all centrally heated. Probably as good an index of success as any.

TEXT 2

At 9.30 a.m., 26 August, AD 2065, the Board, sitting in London, was informed by De Forest that the District of Northern Illinois had riotously cut itself out of all systems and would remain disconnected till the Board should take over and administer it direct.

Every Northern Illinois freight and passenger tower was, he reported, out of action; all District main, local, and guiding lights had been extinguished; all General Communications were dumb, and through traffic had been diverted. No reason had been given, but he gathered unofficially from the Mayor of Chicago that the District complained of 'crowd-making and invasion of privacy'.

As a matter of fact, it is of no importance whether Northern Illinois stay in or out of planetary circuit; as a matter of policy, any complaint of invasion of privacy needs immediate investigation, lest worse follow.

By 9.45 a.m. De Forest, Dragomiroff (Russia), Takahira (Japan), and Pirolo (Italy) were empowered to visit Illinois and 'to take such steps as might be necessary for the resumption of traffic and *all that that implies*'. By 10 a.m. the Hall was empty, and the four Members and I were aboard what Pirolo insisted on calling 'my leetle godchild' – that is to say, the new *Victor Pirolo*. Our Planet prefers to know Victor Pirolo as a gentle, grey-haired enthusiast who spends his time near Foggia, inventing or creating new breeds of Spanish-Italian olive-trees; but there is another side to his nature – the manufacture of quaint inventions, of which the *Victor Pirolo* is, perhaps, not the least surprising. She and a few score sister-craft of the same type embody his latest ideas. But she is not comfortable. An ABC boat does not take the air with the level-keeled lift of a liner, but shoots up rocket-fashion like the 'aeroplane' of our ancestors, and makes her height at top-speed from the first. That is why I found myself sitting suddenly on the large lap of Eustace Arnott, who commands the ABC Fleet. One knows vaguely that there is such a thing as a Fleet somewhere on the Planet, and that, theoretically, it exists for the purposes of what used to be known as 'war'. Only a week before, while visiting a glacier sanatorium behind Gothaven, I had seen some squadrons making false auroras far to the north while they manoeuvred round the Pole; but, naturally, it had never occurred to me that the things could be used in earnest.

___

Solution

TEXT 1

Text 1 mainly uses the simple present tense. This is actually quite unusual and results in the time of narrating and the time of narrative being identical (both are 'now'). Thus, when the narrator remembers his father's visit, and then his childhood, the shift back in time is exactly paralleled by a shift into the simple past ('then'). However, this is a text about Britain in the 1980s – so the present tense is being used to represent past events, while the simple past is used to represent a past which is further back.

actual time	=	recent past	
time of narrating	=	'now'	
time of narrative	=	'now'	(simple present tense)
		'then'	(simple past tense)

TEXT 2

Text 2 uses a range of past-tense forms. This is a more common type of narrative tense structure. The time of narration is *now*, from which we get the present-tense forms of the final paragraph (*Our planet prefers* . . .). In relation to this we get the simple past-tense forms of the *then* of the main narrative (*he reported . . . he gathered . . . Pirolo insisted. . .*), and the *before then* compound phrases which give us the background events (*had riotously cut . . . lights had been extinguished . . . traffic had been diverted* . . .). However, this is a text about the future – so the simple past tense is being used to represent future events, while compound past-tense forms are used to represent events which are *past* from the point of view of the time of narration.

actual time	=	future	
time of narrating	=	'now'	(simple present tense)
time of narrative	=	'then'	(simple past tense)
		'before then'	(compound past tense)

ATTRIBUTION

Text 1   David Lodge, *Nice Work*, pp. 15–16.
Text 2   Rudyard Kipling, 'As Easy as ABC', pp. 33–4.

> Does tense correlate with time-frame? No. Lodge's novel, set in 1980s Britain, is conveyed by the present tense. Kipling's story, set in the future, is conveyed by the past tense. However, both authors shift tense to layer the time-schemes of their narrative. In each case, given the starting point of the tense used for narration, the shifts are internally consistent, but the actual tenses used seem to be irrelevant to the time of the narrated events.

2.3   Simple and compound verb phrases

Note

Section 2.2 shows how writers can use tense shifts to build layered tense structures into their texts, for example:

'tomorrow'	I will see
'now'	I am seeing/I see
'then'	I saw
'before then'	I had seen

This section looks at this in more detail – some of the analysis is complex, and even contentious, but the detail of the analysis is not as important as the overall tendencies shown by the texts.

Definition

Verb phrases can be either simple or complex (compound), finite or non-finite. *Simple* verb phrases have only one verb in them:

I (see)   I (saw)

Complex verb phrases have at least two verb forms. However many there are, the first will always be finite, and the last non-finite:

I (will see)   I (had seen)   I (had been seen)
I (was seeing)   I (haven't seen)

Certain verbs typically add non-finite forms to their right:

I (had intended *to go*)

If there is only one verb in the verb phrase, and it is marked for tense, then it is a simple verb phrase. Complex verb phrases have more than one verb in the verb phrase.

EXAMPLES

Simple verb phrases:

(I)   (woke up)
S   VP

(Nothing)   (happened)
S   VP

(I)   (went back)
S   VP

Compound verb phrases:

(snow)   (had fallen)
S   VP

(cops)   (were eating)
S   VP

(charladies)   (were flicking)
S   VP

Comment

It is common for authors to use both compound and simple verb phrases in a text, and to use the full range of **modals** and auxiliaries. It is less usual to find a text that displays a narrow range, such as only using simple verb phrases, or only using one kind of auxiliary.

TASK

Are the verb phrases in Texts 3, 4 and 5 simple or compound, finite or non-finite?
What are the time-schemes?

TEXT 3

The door was narrow, grilled and topped by a lancet arch. Below the grille there was an iron knocker. I hammered on it.

Nothing happened. I pushed the bell at the side of the door and heard it ring inside not very far off and waited and nothing happened. I worked on the knocker again. Still nothing. I went back up the walk and along to the garage and lifted the door far enough to see that a car with white side-walled tyres was inside. I went back to the front door.

A neat black Cadillac coupé came out of the garage across the way, backed, turned and came along past Lavery's house, slowed, and a thin man in dark glasses looked at me sharply, as if I hadn't any business to be there. I gave him my steely glare and he went on his way.

TEXT 4

I woke up in the Hotel Helsinki at seven the next morning. Someone was coming into my room. The waitress put the tray down beside my bed. Two cups, two saucers, two pots of coffee, two of everything. I tried to look like a man with a friend in the bathroom. The waitress opened the shutters and let the cold northern light fall across my bed. When she had gone I dissolved half a packet of laxative chocolate into each pot of coffee. I rang for room service. A man came. I explained that there was some mistake. The coffee was for the two men down the hall, Mr Seager and Mr Bentley. I gave him their room numbers and a one-mark note. Then I showered, shaved, dressed and checked out of the hotel.

I walked across the street to the first-floor shopping promenade where the charladies were flicking a final mop across the shiny floors of unopened shops. Two fur-hatted cops were eating breakfast in the Columbia Cafe. I took a seat near the window and stared across the square to the Saarinen railway station which dominated the town. More snow had fallen during the night and a small army of shovellers were clearing the bus-park.

I ate my breakfast. Kellogg's *Riisi Muroja* went 'snap, crackle, pop', the eggs were fine and so was the orange juice, but I didn't fancy coffee that morning.

TEXT 5

The baying was behind me now and closer.

Light arced across the land to my left and fixed on the low scrub there. The beam appeared to be bouncing but it was my own movement. The ground was bad for running: the frost had crusted the surface and my feet broke through and were caught by the soft earth beneath. I went down again and lay where I fell, listening to the dogs, awareness of their danger blunted by the body's reluctance to get up and go on: it wanted to lie here with its pain and hunger and thirst, to sleep, so as not to feel them.

The dogs must be under the leash still, their handlers making sure it was a true scent before they slipped them, certain of a kill. They were close now.

I was moving again in a drunken run for the dark, for the trees. Brilliance flooded the field's edge and I saw figures grouped. Men's voices mingled with the crying of the dogs.

Somewhere near the trees I fell again, one shoulder hitting the metaled surface of a road. It was very dark here but the shape of the car was visible, massive above me: I had nearly run into it. It had been waiting here with its lights off so that I wouldn't see it. One of its doors swung open.

She said: 'Get in.'

Solution

TEXT 3

was	(simple)	hammered	(simple)
happened	(simple)	pushed	(simple)
heard	(simple)	ring	(simple)
waited	(simple)	happened	(simple)
working	(simple)	went	(simple)
lifted	(simple)	was	(simple)
went	(simple)	came	(simple)
backed	(simple)	turned	(simple)
came	(simple)	slowed	(simple)
looked	(simple)	had	(simple)
gave	(simple)	went	(simple)

Note: the first verb phrase here presents a difficulty for analysis because the author coordinates *narrow* (an adjective) and *grilled* and *topped* (non-finite verb forms) under *was*. With *narrow*, *was* is a simple main verb; with *grilled* and *topped* it is an auxiliary in a compound verb phrase: an indication that our descriptive grammar is breaking down here.

TEXT 4

woke	(simple)	was coming	(compound)
put	(simple)	tried to look	(compound)
opened	(simple)	let	(simple)
fall	(simple)	had gone	(compound)
dissolved	(simple)	rang	(simple)
came	(simple)	explained	(simple)
was	(simple)	was	(simple)
gave	(simple)	showered	(simple)
shaved	(simple)	dressed	(simple)
checked	(simple)	walked	(simple)
were flicking	(compound)	were eating	(compound)
took	(simple)	stared	(simple)
dominated	(simple)	had fallen	(compound)
were clearing	(compound)	ate	(simple)
went	(simple)	were	(simple)
were	(simple)	was	(simple)
didn't fancy	(compound)		

TEXT 5

was	(simple)	arced	(simple)
fixed	(simple)	appeared	(simple)
to be bouncing	(compound)	was	(simple)
was	(simple)	had crusted	(compound)
broke	(simple)	were caught	(compound)
went	(simple)	lay	(simple)
fell	(simple)	listening	(non-finite)
blunted	(non-finite)	to get up and go on	(non-finite)
wanted	(simple)	to lie	(non-finite)
to sleep	(non-finite)	to feel	(non-finite)
must be	(compound)	making	(non-finite)
was	(simple)	slipped	(simple)
were	(simple)	was moving	(compound)
flooded	(simple)	saw	(simple)
grouped	(non-finite)	mingled	(simple)
fell	(simple)	hitting	(non-finite)
was	(simple)	was	(simple)
had nearly run	(compound)	had been waiting	(compound)

wouldn't see	(compound)	swung	(simple)
said	(simple)	get	(simple)

ATTRIBUTION

Text 3   Raymond Chandler, *The Lady in the Lake*, pp. 18–19.
Text 4   Len Deighton, *Billion-Dollar Brain*, pp. 18–19.
Text 5   Adam Hall, *The Striker Portfolio*, pp. 139–40.

Verdict

Chandler is a very influential writer of detective fiction – not only did he write many novels, which were widely read and transferred to screen, he also had an effect on the style of subsequent writers of detective fiction. Many things characterise his fiction, such as its location in and around Los Angeles, or the way his detective, Philip Marlowe, handles a case. But when considering his linguistic style, one of his hallmarks lies in his treatment of the verb phrase. He uses the simple form far more consistently than other writers.

In Text 3, out of 147 words, there are 23 verb phrases, that is, 16 per cent. One hundred per cent of these are simple verb phrases. It is unusual for a writer to use so many simple verb phrases – indeed, if they do, they run the risk of sounding as if they are trying to parody Chandler. The effect of this frequency of simple verb phrases is to give the texts their matter-of-fact atmosphere. They are full of statements, of events undistanced from the reader by complex time-frames.

Len Deighton also writes thrillers. His style here owes a lot to Chandler. Out of 235 words, 32 are verb phrases, that is, 14 per cent. Out of the 32, 24 are simple, that is, 75 per cent. So we have 16 per cent and 100 per cent for Chandler, and 14 per cent and 75 per cent for Deighton. You might think that this is not particularly close, but compare the figures for a third thriller writer, Adam Hall. Hall uses a range of complex and simplex verb phrases in Text 5, and this is the unmarked, default norm for authors. If we compare his frequencies, we find that out of 235 words, 40 are verb phrases, that is, 17 per cent. Out of the 40, 17 are simple, that is, 42 per cent. Table 2.1 below compares the simple/complex frequencies of all three authors:

TABLE 2.1 Verb phrases in Chandler, Deighton and Hall

	Chandler	Deighton	Hall
Verb phrases (as a percentage of total words)	16%	14%	17%
Simple verbs (as a percentage of total words)	100%	75%	42%

The three authors use about the same number of verb phrases, that is, between 17 per cent and 14 per cent; but they vary as to how many of these are simple. In this respect Deighton is more like Chandler than he is like Hall.

Deighton's writing is similar to Chandler's in other respects. Compare the structure of the last two sentences in Deighton's text:

> I ate my breakfast. Kellogg's *Riisi Muroja* went 'snap, crackle, pop', the eggs were fine and so was the orange juice, but I didn't fancy coffee that morning.

with the last three sentences in another novel by Chandler:

> I rode down to the street floor and went out on the steps of the City Hall. It was a cool day and very clear. You could see a long way – but not as far as Velma had gone.
> (Raymond Chandler, *Farewell, My Lovely*, p. 253)

Both of these texts show a sequence of simple sentences containing main clauses and coordinated main clauses, with no subordination. Both contain ellipsis ('the eggs were fine and so was the orange juice'; 'it was a cool day and very clear'), and both end with a *but* negator which appears to contrast the final clause with its immediate precedent, although in fact the contrast is with something that has happened earlier in the text.

Overall, Hall uses a much more complex set of tense and verb forms, even though, like the first two texts, it is a narrative of past events which uses the simple past as its main tense. Where Text 4 sets up a contrast between the continuous actions of minor characters, and the once-only, completed actions of the narrator, in an unambiguous past, Text 5 is more immediate in its narrative – and the narrator is depicted as being much more involved with the actions he narrates.

Chandler and Deighton's heroes are very much in control of the situations in which they find themselves – and the rigid separation of time of narrating ('now' – implicit present) from time of narrative ('then' – past-tense forms) underlines this. Hall's hero, however, is in a life-threatening situation, and much of the tension comes from our ability to share his uncertainty (which he felt at the time of narrative, but cannot feel at the time of narrating) of survival.

By definition, a past-tense, first-person narrative implies that the narrator has survived whatever danger he or she may face to live up to the time of narrating. This could undermine any attempt by a thriller writer to create tension. One way round this is to have the narrative in present tense – but this is an unusual form, and therefore intrusive. Hall therefore employs a series of devices which serve to collapse the distinction between the time of narrating and the time of the narrative – devices which serve to bring the narrative events into the present. This can be seen in the first sentence:

> The baying was behind me now and closer.

where a past-tense verb (*was*) **collocates** with (appears close to) a present adverbial (*now*). Here the tense encodes the time of narrating as 'now', while the adverb encodes the time of narrative as 'now': the narrator becomes both experiencer and interpreter.

Similar collocations come with *wanted* and *here* (rather than *there*), and *must be ... still ... were ... now ....* The text merges the two temporal points of view (narrating past events and experiencing present ones), and constructs a much more gripping narrative as a result.

A further feature of this 'now/then' merger is the use of tenseless non-finite clauses to provide a background to the completed, simple past-tense actions of the main narrative (non-finite verbs in italics; see also Section 2.9):

> the beam appeared *to be bouncing* but it was my own movement . . .
> I went down again and lay where I fell, *listening to* the dogs, awareness of their danger *blunted* by the body's reluctance *to get up* and *go on* . . .
> it wanted *to lie* here with its pain and hunger and thirst, *to sleep* so as not *to feel* them making sure . . .
> I fell again, one shoulder *hitting* the metaled surface of the road . . .

Here, the finite verbs are all simple past tense (*appeared, went, fell*), but note that they could be any tense at all, without affecting the non-finite forms:

the beam appears to be bouncing
I go down again and lie where I fall, listening . . .
It wants to lie here

Use of the non-finite forms therefore allows the narrative to be less specific about its temporal reference, and preserves the 'now/then' paradox.

CONCLUSION

These three texts show writers building tense structures in their texts of increasing complexity for different ends. The **tense/aspect** system in English is formidably complicated, and is capable of surprising combinations, for example the 'now' plus past-tense narrative.

2.4 Uses of the present tense

Definition

There are only two morphological tenses in English: simple past, and simple present (*morphological* here means that words change their forms to indicate meaning). For example:

I see (present)   I *saw* (past)
I walk (present)   I *walked* (past)

All of the other tenses are formed, not by changing the shape of the verb, but by adding auxiliary verbs to the verb phrase or by using adverbs:

I *will* see
will = auxiliary
I go *tomorrow*
tomorrow = adverb
I *had* seen
had = auxiliary

We commonly assume that the tense of a verb tells us when the action it refers to takes, took, or will take place, but in fact there is not a one-to-one relationship between tense and time:

I leave for Brisbane at one.

where a present-tense verb refers to future time.

It is important therefore to keep the notions of tense and time apart if we want to be accurate in how we analyse texts.

For example, it is not true that the English present tense exclusively, or even mostly, refers to events which are actually happening at the time of speaking or writing. There are at least five possible uses of the present tense:

1   Habitual action: *I buy the* Guardian *every day.*
2   General truth: *Tromsø is inside the Arctic Circle.*
3   Narration of past events: *So she comes up to me and says* ...
4   As-it-happens narrative: *Beardsley crosses to Cole, and it's a goal.*
5   Future: *I fly to Helsinki at eleven.*

Note that (4) is highly restricted to the world of TV and radio commentary – in fact a more frequent way of dealing with events as they happen is to use a compound verb phrase consisting of *be* as an auxiliary, plus the *-ing* form of the main verb:

6   As-it-happens narrative: *I'm speaking to you from Sandra's house* ...

TASK

Note the present-tense forms in this text: are they habitual, general truth, simple present, *be + -ing*? How do they pattern?

TEXT 6

Come back, come back, come back . . .

This is the effort, the enormous effort, under which the human brain cracks.

But not before the thing is done, not before the mountain moves.

He hesitates. He stops. I have him.

'Listen. You hear me now, don't you? It's quite early – not twelve yet. The door will still be open. All you've got to do is walk upstairs. If anybody speaks to you, say: "The woman in number forty-one, she expects me; she's waiting for me." Say that.'

I see him, very clearly, in my head. I daren't let him go for a moment.

Come back, come back, come back . . . .

He mustn't have to knock, I think. He must be able to walk straight in.

I get up and try to put the key on the outside of the door. I drop it. I leave the door a little open.

'I've got all my clothes on,' I think. 'How stupid!'

I undress very quickly. I am watching every step he takes.

Now he is turning into the end of the street. Very clear he is in my head. He is turning into the end of my street. I see the houses . . . .

I get into bed. I lie there trembling. I am very tired. Not me, no. Don't worry, it's my *sale cerveau* that's so tired. Don't worry about that – no more *sale cerveau*.

I think: 'How awful I must look! I must put the light out.'

But it doesn't matter. Now I am simple and not afraid; now I am myself. He can look at me if he wants to. I'll only say: 'You see, I cried like that because you went away.'

(Or did I cry like that because I'll never sing again, because the light in my *sale cerveau* has gone out?)

He presses the button and the door opens.

He is coming up the stairs.

Now the door is moving, the door is opening wide. I put my arm over my eyes.

He comes in. He shuts the door after him.

I lie very still, with my arm over my eyes. As still as if I were dead . . . .

I don't need to look. I know.

I think: 'Is it the blue dressing-gown, or the white one? That's very important. I must find that out – it's very important.' I take my arm away from my eyes. It is the white dressing-gown.

He stands there, looking down at me. Not sure of himself, his mean eyes flickering.

He doesn't say anything. Thank God, he doesn't say anything. I look straight into his eyes and despise another poor devil of a human being for the last time. For the last time . . . .

Then I put my arms round him and pull him down on to the bed, saying: 'Yes – yes – yes . . . .

ATTRIBUTION

Jean Rhys, *Good Morning Midnight*, pp. 475–6.

Verdict

This is the closing section of Jean Rhys's novel, *Good Morning Midnight*. In this section we move between most of the possible uses of present tense. First the passage has a general truth usage (*cracks ... moves*), but this quickly shifts into as-it-happens narrative ('He hesitates . . .') as the narrator tries to will the man to return to her.

The remainder of the passage builds a contrast between the man's imagined return and the narrator's thoughts and reactions by using *be* plus *-ing* for the return ('he is turning . . .') contrasted with simple present ('I get into bed'). Thus, even though everything is presented as being in the present, aspect is used to separate the two lines of action.

Present-tense narrative implies a lack of distance between the narrator and the events. The use of the present tense to narrate past events adds immediacy to the telling. In this passage, the lack of distance adds to our impression of the narrator as emotionally and psychologically unstable, and not really in control. Imagine the passage rewritten in the past tense: the narrator would immediately appear more in control, and the events more distant.

In fact, the *he* pronouns in this passage refer to two different men: one the narrator imagines returning to her; and one who actually enters her room wearing a white dressing gown. This is never made fully explicit in the novel. The combination of the pronoun *he* with two referents, and the use of the present tense without consistent shifting to the past, together cause a certain amount of processual difficulty for the reader. If we have no names and no tense shifting between interior discourse and narrative, then it's not easy to follow. The author is presenting a character who has precisely this difficulty; she isn't really able to comprehend her intimate relationships. Rather than making it up with the person with whom she seems to have just quarrelled, the speaker makes it up with the next person to walk in the room.

Jean Rhys presents a character who is not coping with social interaction and not able to forge relationships of any substance – she can't target her actions. However she acts and whatever she does, applies equally to whoever she comes into contact with. She's unable to select whatever is suitable behaviour in a given circumstance. This is conveyed to us partly by her unremitting use of the present tense. She can get no perspective on events: they just happen to her.

2.5   The passive

Definition

Turning a verb from active to passive involves a change of word order, the addition of the verb *be* and, optionally, a *by* + subject phrase.

TEST-FRAME

I ____ something = active
Something ____ ____ (by me) = passive

EXAMPLES

I saw something = active
Something was seen (by me) = passive
I tidied it away = active
It has been tidied away (by me) = passive
I bonfired a lot = active
A lot had been bonfired (by me) = passive
I may view them = active
They may be viewed (by me) = passive

Comment

If a verb is presented in the passive, then the subject of that verb can be concealed by omitting the *by* phrase, as occurs in Text 7. Consistent use of the passive may sometimes give a formal effect, as for example in scientific writing (e.g. *the test tube was filled with a 30% salt solution*), where the purpose is to focus attention away from the subject. In political language, use of the passive can express concern without responsibility:

Something must be done.

(with the unspoken implication: *But I'm not going to say who by*), or can present as inevitable something which is in fact a matter of opinion and/or questionable:

Inflation must be beaten.

TASK

> Identify the passive verb constructions in Text 7.
> What or who is the subject of the verb?

TEXT 7 ━━━━━━━━━━━━━━━━━━━━━━━━━━━━━━━━━━━━

I'm finding out that a lot of what I thought had been bonfired, Oxfam-ed, used for land-fill, has in fact been tidied away in sound archives, stills libraries, image banks, memorabilia mausoleums, tat troves, mug morgues.

It's an odd experience to find yourself catalogued, card-indexed, museumised, a speck of data for the information professionals to bounce around.

It seems that as long as you're in print or on film or a name on a buff envelope in an archive somewhere, you're never truly dead now. You can be electronically colourised, emulsified, embellished, enhanced, coaxed towards some state of virtual reality.

You can be reactivated or reembodied; simulated and hologrammed. In just the last two years my voice has been artificially reprocessed for stereo effect and reincarnated in half-speed remasterings and on digital compact-disc.

The spare-parts that make this possible are housed in a proliferating number of noninvasive environments in London, where they may be viewed (fingered, sniffed, listened to) by appointment.

Solution

had been bonfired . . . land-fill
has been tidied away
can be colourised . . . coaxed
can be reactivated . . . hologrammed
has been reprocessed . . . reincarnated
are housed
may be viewed

ATTRIBUTION

Gordon Burn, *Alma Cogan*, p. 165.

Verdict

This passage reports the narrator's discovery that her voice has been archived by various electronic means. It is no longer 'her' voice – she has no control over when it is played, or who listens to it. By suppressing the subject of the verbs, all these things just seem to happen inevitably, of their own volition.

The narrator of this text is a researcher into her own life, ploughing through theatrical museums and archives in London. A feature of personhood is an ability to act on your surroundings – to affect things, to do things, to function as the subject of an active verb. A feature of a museum exhibit, or a record in an archive, is its inactivity: things are done to it (preservation, consultation, cataloguing).

In this text, the transformation of a person into a set of museum pieces is represented in the series of passive constructions. In the context of this novel, which reincarnates the (once real but now actually dead) 1950s/1960s singer Alma Cogan, and has her investigate her own life, the use of the passive enacts the dehumanising effects of celebrity in the twentieth century.

2.6   The imperative

Definition

The imperative is the part of the verb that is used to give commands or instructions, for example,

Keep off the grass.
Turn right.
Don't do that.
Wash your hands.

Sometimes the noun or pronoun is included, but it need not be:

You! Come here!
Hughie, stop playing football and come and do some work.

Comment

The imperative usually sounds as if it has the force of a command or order. Therefore, some speakers may try to avoid it, in order to avoid giving offence. It is usual, for example, when ordering a meal in Britain, to use forms other than the imperative, for example: *I'd like the fish, please* or *Could I have the fish?*, because the imperative (*Bring me fish*, or *Give me the fish*) sounds too bold and rude. Instructions usually use the imperative mood, so a knitting pattern, for example, will read: *Knit one, purl one*. But when teaching a knitting class, a teacher may avoid the imperative and say, for example: *and the next step is to knit one, purl one*, or *and at this point we knit one, purl one*. Imperatives are a feature of written texts rather than spoken discourse, unless the speaker doesn't mind causing offence.

Text 8 purports to be a cookery recipe, but you may prefer to regard it as a work of fiction. The narrator is instructing the reader how to make a dish called *farce double*, as made in the French village of La Tour Lambert.

Identify the imperatives in Text 8.
What is their force and function?

TEXT 8

To a saucepan filled with 2½ cups of cold water, add salt, pepper, 2 pinches of grated nutmeg and 6 tbsp of butter. Boil. Off heat, begin stirring in 2½ cups of flour and continue as you again bring the water to a boil. Take off heat. Beat in 5 eggs, one at a time, then 5 egg whites. Let the liquid cool.

Earlier, you will have ground 3¾ lbs of fish with a mortar and pestle – heads, tails, bones, and all – and forced them through a coarse sieve. Do *not* use a grinder, blender, or cuisinart. The sieve of La Tour Lambert is an elegant sock of meshed copper wire, with a fitted ashwood plunger. It is kept immaculately bright. Its apertures are shrewdly gauged to crumble the bones without pulverizing the flesh. Into the strained fish, mix small amounts of salt, white pepper, nutmeg, and chopped truffles – fresh ones, if possible. (See TRUFFLE).

Stir fish and liquid into an even paste.

Two hours before, you will have refrigerated 1 cup of the heaviest cream available. Here, of course, access to a cow is a blessing.

The breathtakingly viscid cream of La Tour Lambert is kept in specially excavated cellars. Those without one use the town chiller, in the middle depths – cool but not cold – of the cave mentioned earlier. Often I have watched the attendant women entering and emerging from that room, dusky figures in cowls, shawls, and long gray gowns, bearing earthenware jugs like offerings to a saint.

Beat the cool cream into the paste. Do it slowly: think of those erect, deliberate Auvergnat women as they stand in the faint gloom of the cave, beating with gestures of timeless calm. It should take at least 15 minutes to complete the task.

At some previous moment, you will have made the stuffing for the quenelles. (This is what makes the stuffing 'double'). It consists of the milt of the fish and the sweetbreads of the lamb, both the neck and the stomach varieties. (Don't forget to mention *them* to your butcher). The milt is rapidly blanched. The sweetbreads are diced, salted, spiced with freshly ground hot pepper, and tossed for 6 minutes in clarified butter. Both are then chopped very fine (blender permitted) and kneaded into an unctuous mass with the help of 1 cup of lamb marrow and 3 tbsp of aged Madeira.

I said at the outset that I am in favor of appropriate substitutions in preparing *farce double*: but even though one eminent authority has suggested it, stuffing the quenelles with banana peanut butter is not appropriate.

The quenelles must now be shaped. Some writers who have discoursed at length on the traditional Auvergnat shape urge its adoption at all costs. I disagree. For the inhabitants of La Tour Lambert, who attach great significance to *farce double*, it may be right to feel strongly on this point. The same cannot be said for families in Maplewood or Orange County. You have enough to worry about as it is. If you are, however, an incurable stickler, you should know that in Auvergne molds are used. They are called *beurdes* (they are, coincidentally, shaped like birds), and they are available here. You can find them in any of the better head shops.

But forget about bird molds. Slap your fish paste onto a board and roll it flat. Spread on stuffing in parallel ½-inch bands 2 inches apart. Cut paste midway between bands, roll these strips into cylinders, and slice the cylinders into sections no larger than a small headache. Dip each piece in truffle crumbs. (See TRUFFLE).

I refuse to become involved in the pros and cons of presteaming the quenelles. The only steam in La Tour Lambert is a rare fragrant wisp from the dampened fire of a roasting pit.

We now approach a crux in the preparation of *farce double*: enveloping the quenelles and binding them into the lamb. I must make a stern observation here; and you must listen to it. You must take it absolutely to heart.

If the traditional ways of enveloping the quenelles are arduous, they are in no way gratuitous. On them depends an essential component of *farce double*, namely the subtle interaction of lamb and fish. While the quenelles (and the poaching liquid that bathes them) must be largely insulated from the encompassing meat, they should not be wholly so. The quenelles must not be drenched in roasting juice or the lamb in fishy broth, but an exchange should occur, definite no matter how mild. Do not *under any circumstance* use a baggie or Saran Wrap to enfold the quenelles. Of course it's easier. So are TV dinners. For once, demand the utmost of yourself: the satisfaction will astound you, and *there is no other way.*

Solution

IMPERATIVES

add, boil, begin, continue, take, beat, let, do not use, mix, stir, beat, do, think, don't forget, forget, slap, roll, spread, cut, roll, slice, dip, do not . . . use, demand

ATTRIBUTION

Harry Mathews, 'Country Cooking from Central France: Roast Boned Rolled Stuffed Shoulder of Lamb (*farce double*)', pp. 22–3.

Verdict

Usually, in cookery recipes, most verbs are in the imperative form, and there are a lot of them. They do not give offence, because the reader is at liberty to ignore them! (You don't have to cook in the way suggested unless you want to.) So the imperatives in a cookery recipe, or knitting pattern, or car manual, or whatever, don't have the force of causing fear in the listener. This is unlike, for example, traffic signs. They use the imperative (*Turn right, Go slow, Stop*) and their unwritten message is 'If you don't turn right here, you'll be liable to a fine.' Compare this to a parent speaking to a child: 'Come here and be quiet.' The child knows that the unspoken corollary of these imperatives is '... or else I will inflict some painful form of torture upon you!' There is a difference between those imperatives which cause fear, or offence, in the listener (and hence must be obeyed); and those which the listener can safely ignore should they so wish.

Harry Mathews adheres to the traditional cookery recipe style by using imperatives. But he deviates from the normal format by (a) introducing digressions; (b) introducing the first-person singular; (c) by altering the usual tense sequence (i.e. 'first Step 1, then Step 2, then Step 3'), and (d) by giving some of his imperatives the force of commands, rather than instructions:

> Do *not* use a grinder, blender, or cuisinart.
> Beat the cool cream into the paste. Do it slowly.
> Do not *under any circumstance* use a baggie or Saran Wrap.

Taken with his exhortation 'I must make a stern observation here; and you must listen to it. You must take it absolutely to heart', Mathews addresses the reader as though the reader has no free will, and has to obey. Of course, this isn't really the case, and hence the humorous effect of the text.

2.7   Non-finite verb forms: '*to* + base' form (the infinitive)

Definition

This is the part of the verb traditionally known as the **infinitive**. It is the non-finite, undeclined form of the verb.

TEST-FRAME

He wanted to _____ the syringe

EXAMPLES

to squirt
to prod
to start

Exercises

Identify the infinitives in the following:

1   hardly daring to breathe

2   naughty to play with flies

3   It had thus to be done quickly

Comment

The base form of *be* + *to* can combine with the past participle to form the passive voice. The passive serves to obscure the subject of the verb, as in (3). In Exercises (1)–(3), the narrator is about to kill a fly (see Text 9), so the passive construction hides his responsibility for the act of killing.

TASK

Identify the *to* + base forms in the texts.
What is their effect when used in non-finite sentences?

TEXT 9

To hold the syringe gently, firmly but delicately – not to squirt, but to prod the sleeper into wakefulness with the nozzle, taking care to start no abrupt flight of fear. Only to stir a movement, to initiate a presence from such a deep dead sleep. Gently, gently – lean thus into the ivy, face close in to the leaves, bowed in yet hardly daring to breathe, not to shake a single leaf, hand held far away up the wall, but face now close, secret, smelling the earth underneath the ivy like a smell close to earlier days, intimate the eyes and closed the world . . . then carefully prod, no tickle – tickle the long dead leg on the leaf. But still this curious fly slept on. I bend closer, risking a cramp, tautening round the brass syringe my pale, large-looking fingers. Somewhere overhead was the afternoon, spread out wide and calm – there was a pale clear May sky overhead. Four o'clock the hour – the edge-hour before tea. No one about. People everywhere resting. So that down by the ivy I was secure, nothing to disturb the secret moment. That squat syringe filled with brown glutinous killer armed me powerfully; still – it was forbidden, naughty to play with flies, embarrassing an adult to be uncovered at such play. It had thus to be done quickly, before anyone saw. Yet this perverse fly remained fast asleep! It might be dead already! There on the dark ivy leaf how still, its long leather-jacket legs firmly hooked into place.

TEXT 10

Before this delirium, freedom, justice, equality and brotherhood melted away into spectral absurdity. The only genuine desire left was the desire to destroy.

To wreak vengeance. To tear down. To burn. To loot. To insult. To kill. The President and the men who surrounded him understood perfectly. They were not led astray by spectres: they were realists. And, most important of all, the void and hunger were within them too. Cheated out of a self, the mob would not be cheated out of its anguish.

Solution

TEXT 9

to hold, to squirt, to prod, to start, to stir, to initiate, to breathe, to shake, to disturb, to play, to be, to be

TEXT 10

to destroy, to wreak, to tear, to burn, to loot, to insult, to kill

ATTRIBUTION

Text 9   William Sansom, *The Body*, p. 1.
Text 10   Shiva Naipaul, *A Hot Country*, p. 185.

Verdict

TEXT 9

This is the opening passage of the novel, and because the infinitive is not marked for tense or person, we can't tell when the first paragraph is set. Are *lean* and *prod* further infinitives with *to* omitted, or are they imperatives (the inner voice of the narrator commanding himself?) – in which case the passage is present tense. Does the past participle *held* imply a past auxiliary (*was held*) or a present auxiliary (*is held*)? The author has used *to* + base forms in non-finite clauses in this passage to indicate interior thought, possibly because interior thought need not be marked for tense, person or number – the thinker knows these things already. He wants to kill the fly, but not while it sleeps, as that would be no fun. He needs it to wake up so that he can be sure it feels pain before it dies. The thinker is dissembling – even to himself. He changes the base form *prod* to the euphemism, *tickle*, and feels embarrassment at the thought of discovery. Obscuring the agency of the verb enables him to both torture the fly and pretend to himself that he isn't really torturing it.

TEXT 10

Here the *to* + base forms are in a finite clause, despite the punctuation and layout. Therefore the sentence is marked for tense and number: the subject is *desire*, the finite verb is *was* (past tense, singular), and the *to* + base forms all modify the complement (the second *desire*). They act as postmodifiers in the noun phrase *the desire to* .... The effect on reading through all these modifiers is to evoke the ungovernability of the mob, as the reader gets further and further from the head of the noun phrase which governs the modifiers. By the time the reader reaches *to insult, to kill*, the head desire is no longer foremost in the memory, and so these infinitives appear to stand alone rather than depend upon the head. The syntax creates the escalating or snowballing effect ascribed in the text to anarchy.

2.8 Non-finite verb forms: '*-ing*' forms

Definition

Verbs are either finite or non-finite. Finite verbs have tense (*I laugh<u>ed</u>*) and agree with the subject (*I write_, she write<u>s</u>*). Non-finite verbs lack both of these.

There are three non-finite forms of the verb: the *-ing* form, the infinitive, and the past participle (which often ends in *-ed*). It may seem strange to say that *-ing* forms and past participles do not carry tense, but this can be shown to be the case by the following examples:

I am going.
I will be going.
I was going.

I am tired.

I was tired.
I will be tired.

where the non-finite form of the verb is accompanied by a finite auxiliary form which carries the tense – as the tense changes, the non-finite form remains the same.

We can give similar examples for the infinitive:

I am to go.
I will have to go.
I was to go.

Non-finite forms can either appear with finite auxiliaries in finite verb phrases as above, or on their own in non-finite clauses:

(Told of the accident), I hurried to the scene.
(Hoping against hope), they opened the newspaper.
All he wanted was (to be a footballer).

Again, note that the tense of the verb in the main clause is irrelevant to the non-finite verb.

This lack of tense and subject means that non-finite forms often have a general tone – the events or states they refer to could happen, could have happened, or may happen any time, to anyone. In contrast, finite forms are more specific.

TASK

Read the following text.
  Now identify the finite and non-finite verb forms.
  Why do they pattern as they do?

TEXT 11

And morning after morning, all over the immense, damp, dreary town and the packing-case colonies of huts in the suburb allotments, young men were waking up to another workless empty day to be spent as they could best contrive; selling boot-laces, begging, playing draughts in the hall of the Labour Exchange, hanging about urinals, opening the doors of cars, helping with crates in the markets, gossiping, lounging, stealing, overhearing racing tips, sharing stumps of cigarette-ends picked up in the gutter, singing folk-songs for groschen in courtyards and between stations in the carriages of the Underground Railway. After the New Year, the snow fell, but did not lie; there was no money to be earned by sweeping it away. The shopkeepers rang all the coins on the counter for fear of the forgers. Frl. Schroeder's astrologer foretold the end of the world. 'Listen,' said Fritz Wendel, between sips of a cocktail in the bar of the Eden Hotel, 'I give a damn if this country goes communist. What I mean, we'd have to alter our ideas a bit. Hell, who cares?'

Solution

The passage opens with a run of non-finite *-ing* forms: one (*waking*) as part of a finite verb phrase, the rest as part of non-finite clauses. It ends with a series of finite simple past-tense verbs.

> *Non-finite*
> waking, selling, begging, playing, hanging, opening, helping, gossiping, lounging, stealing, overhearing, sharing, singing, sweeping

> *Finite*
> were, fell, did, was, rang, foretold, said

ATTRIBUTION

Christopher Isherwood, *Mr Norris Changes Trains*, p. 109.

This novel is set in inter-war Germany, and is documenting political changes, though in an indirect way. Instead of stating directly that Hitler's rise to power occurred during an economic depression, Isherwood presents everyday life in Berlin, showing how it is affected by economic concerns. New Year is seen as an economic and political watershed.

The text marks this watershed with a shift from non-finite verbs to simple past-tense, finite forms. In the first section there is a sense of timelessness, repetition, the dulling effect of the depression; in the second time is differentiated – something has changed with the New Year. The narrator is no longer part of the events, is distanced from them, they have finished. In the first section the narrator is part of the events (even though they are nominally past-tense) – by virtue of the indefinite non-finite verbs. Individual activities are presented as if they are part of one larger activity – unemployment. In the second section, the narrator stops aligning himself with the generic concept of passing the time, and focuses on the new, fatalistic mood of named individuals. Thus the non-finite verbs convey a generic collectivity, while the finite verbs anchor the depression to individual characters. Things are going from bad to worse.

2.9 Non-finite verb forms: time and tense

As we said in Section 2.1, verb phrases can be divided into finite phrases, which have tense and person/number agreement, and non-finite phrases, which do not. Tense and person/number agreement can be tested for, for example:

> Sophie opened the door without a backward glance.

Here the verb phrase is *opened*, and this can be shifted from past to present tense:

> Sophie *opens* the door without a backward glance.

We can also now test for person/number agreement by changing the subject:

> They *open* the door without a backward glance.

So this verb phrase is finite because it has tense and person/number agreement.

Non-finite verbs lack these specific references to tense and person, and it is this that makes them useful to writers, and significant in stylistic analysis. In the following sentence, one of the verb phrases is finite, one non-finite:

> So stepping over the threshold into the hall she was stepping over that sack of work tools.

Whatever the tense of the second verb phrase, the first will always consist of just *stepping*, for example:

> So *stepping* over the threshold into the hall she *is* stepping over that sack of work tools.

and,

> So *stepping* over the threshold into the hall she *will be* stepping over that sack of work tools.

and,

> So *stepping* over the threshold into the hall she *stepped* over that sack of work tools.

Although common sense might try to tell us that the *-ing* form on *stepping* makes it present tense here, we in fact interpret the time reference in the context of the other verb – it can be either past, present or future. If we didn't have that context, the non-finite verb would be timeless.

Identify the finite and non-finite verb phrases in the following text.
     What is the relationship between tense and/or finiteness and time?

TEXT 12

Sophie opened the door without a backward glance at the group or at the godchild huddled on the stool so mournful and forlorn. The child Sophie grieved for took another form altogether. So stepping over the threshold into the hall she was stepping over that sack of work tools by his bedroom door again, a heavy gray canvas sack spilling out before enemy eyes – screwdriver, syringe, clockworks, dynamite. She looked out into the hall of the Southwest Community Infirmary, fresh white paint dizzying her, temples buzzing, eyes stinging. Smitty.

Smitty climbing the leg of the statue. The other students running down the street waving banners made from sheets. Mrs. Taylor watching from the window, leaning on pillows she'd made from rally banners. Smitty on the arm of the war hero chanting 'Hell, no, we won't go.' Sirens scattering the marchers. TV cameras and trucks shoving through the crowd. Mrs. Taylor screaming in the window. A boy face down in the street, his book bag flattened. The police rushing the statue like a tank. The package up under Smitty's arm. The other flung across the hind of the first brass horse. The blow that caught him in the shins.

Sophie face down in the jailhouse bed springs. Portland Edgers, her neighbor, handed a billy club. The sheriff threatening.

Mrs. Taylor moaning in the window. The boy gagging on his own blood face down in the street, the cameras on him. Smitty with a bull horn. A Black TV announcer misnumbering the crowd, mixmatching the facts, lost to the community. Smitty. The blow that caught him in the groin.

The blow that caught her in the kidney. Someone howling in the next cell. A delegation from the church out front talking reasonably. Sophie face down on the jailhouse bed springs, the rusty metal cutting biscuits out of her cheeks.

Smitty kicking at the clubs, the hands. Smitty jammed between the second brass horse and the flagpole. The package balanced in the crook of the bayonet. The blow that caught him from behind.

Portland Edgers turning on the sheriff and wrestled down on her back and beaten. Sophie mashed into the springs. Portland Edgers screaming into her neck.

Smitty pulled down against the cement pedestal, slammed against the horses' hooves, dragged on his stomach to the van. A boot in his neck. Child. Four knees in his back. Son. The package ripped from his grip. The policeman racing on his own path and none other's. The man, the statue going up Pegasus. Manes, hooves, hinds, the brass head of some dead soldier and a limb of one once-live officer airborne over city hall. A flagpole buckling at the knees.

And a tall building tottering trembling falling down inside her face down in the jailhouse bed springs teeth splintering and soul groaning. Smitty. Edgers. Reverend Michaels in the corridor being reasonable.

Sophie Heywood closed the door of the treatment room. And there was something in the click of it that made many of the old-timers, veterans of the incessant war – Garveyites, Southern Tenant Associates, trade unionists, Party members, Pan-Africanists – remembering night riders and day traitors and the cocking of guns, shudder.

ATTRIBUTION

Toni Cade Bambara, *The Salt Eaters*, pp. 14–15.

Verdict

This passage opens and closes in the simple past tense so often used for narrative in novels ('Sophie *opened* ...' 'Sophie Heywood *closed* ... there *was* something in the click of it that *made* ...'). If we want to maintain a tense–time relationship, we can justify this use of past tense by thinking of a 'now' of narrating in which we are being told, or are reading the story. From the point of view of this time of narrating, events such as Sophie opening the door happen in the past: the time of narrative.

The lack of a one-to-one relationship between tense and the time at which events happen is made clear in this passage. It begins with simple and continuous past-tense forms (simple: 'Sophie grieved'; continuous: 'she was stepping over ...') and then moves into a sequence of remembered past events expressed in non-finite *-ing* and past-participle forms ('Smitty *climbing* the leg of the statue. The other students *running* down the street ...' 'Smitty *kicking* at the clubs, the hands. Smitty *jammed* between the second brass horse and flagpole').

The use of non-finite forms for narration of past events here has a significant effect on the narrative. Note that these forms (from the second paragraph onwards) do not have the usual context of finite forms (which *is* provided for the non-finite forms in the first paragraph). These forms are thus effectively placed outside the tense structure of the narrative – although we can tell that the events they relate to are at two removes from the time of narrating. Bambara thus avoids the distancing effect tense relationships can have, and creates the impression that her narrator is experiencing these events for the first time as she narrates them.

Expressed in non-finite forms, outside the tense structure of the piece, the events are presented as a series of vivid images. If we rewrite the passage using finite forms, much of this vividness is lost:

> Smitty was climbing the leg of the statue. The other students were running down the street waving banners made from sheets. Mrs. Taylor watched from the window, leaning on pillows she'd made from rally banners. Smitty was on the arm of the war hero chanting 'Hell, no, we won't go.' Sirens scattered the marchers. TV cameras and trucks shoved through the crowd. Mrs. Taylor screamed in the window. A boy was face down in the street, his book bag flattened. The police rushed the statue like a tank. The package was up under Smitty's arm. The other was flung across the hind of the first brass horse. The blow that caught him in the shins.

Here the more explicit tense structure distances the reader and the narrator from the events. Bambara is an experimental novelist – here she presents several characters experiencing extreme pain simultaneously. By using non-finite verbs, she challenges the reader to sort out which character is experiencing which event. The reader momentarily undergoes confusion and disorientation as the characters undergo chaos and pain.

•   •   •

Chapter 3

The Clause

- 3.1   Introduction to syntax   90
- 3.2   Analysing clause structure   94
- 3.3   The relationship between S and V   98
- 3.4   Relative size of syntactic elements:
         light X elements   102
- 3.5   Obligatory X elements (transitivity)   109
- 3.6   Expansion of X elements   112
- 3.7   Heavy S and X elements before
         the verb   116
- 3.8   Placement of adverbials in the clause   120
- 3.9   Main clauses   124
- 3.10   Coordination   133
- 3.11   Subordination and the sentence   140
- 3.12   Ambiguity in syntax   142
- 3.13   Prepositions   147
- 3.14   Interrogatives   156

3.1 Introduction to syntax

When noun and verb phrases function together, they form clauses. The simplest types of clause consist of a noun phrase, a verb phrase and an optional third element (labelled as X):

NP(...) VP(...) X(...)

The first noun phrase is usually the **subject** (the person or thing which does the verb):

SubjectNP(Bond) VP(ate) X(the delicious meal)

SubjectNP(Sophie) VP(opened) X(the door)

SubjectNP(The child Sophie grieved for) VP(took) X(another form)

The X element will either be an **object/complement** (O/C: in which case it will often be a noun phrase, or an adjectival phrase (AdjP)):

NP(Bond) VP(ate) O/C NP(the delicious meal)

NP(the Turkish coffee) VP(was) O/C AdjP(jet black)

or it will be an **adverbial** (Av) element – a clause or phrase which tells us something about the how, where or when of some aspect of the clause, and which can be moved around or deleted:

X Av(For ten minutes) NP(Bond) VP(stood)

NP(Bond) VP(stood) X Av(for ten minutes)

NP(Bond) VP(stood)

Sometimes, X will consist of both object/complement and an adverbial:

NP(Bond)   VP(ate)   X   O/C(the delicious meal)   Av(on a table)

We do not need to distinguish between the object and the complement for stylistic analysis, but the mobility of the adverbial element means that it can be useful to separate it from the object or the complement.

The normal order of these elements in English clauses is SVX, but this can sometimes be disrupted for stylistic effect. The most essential part of the clause, that which cannot be deleted) is VP (the verb phrase), for example: *Sit!*, *Heel!*, *Lie down!*.

Information: given and new

Just as clauses tend to begin with subjects, and move on through verbs to an X element, so we have expectations about the type of information clauses present us with. We expect the first piece of information to be familiar to us (to be 'given'), and the last to be unfamiliar ('new'):

given NP(Bond) VP(stood and gazed out) *new* X(across the sparkling water barrier between Europe and Asia)

Here *Bond* is given because we have come across the name before in the story, while *the sparkling water barrier* is new as this is the first time it has been mentioned. The tendency for given information to come at the start of a clause and new at the end is no more than that: a tendency. Writers can, and often do, disrupt our expectations (for example, to create tension by withholding information).

Since given information tends to come at the beginning of clauses, it can be said that the subject noun phrase in most clauses will refer to given information. Since new information tends to come at the end, the likelihood is that the X element will contain new information.

S NP(...)   VP(...)   X(...)
given   new

This structural tendency has a further consequence: if something is given information, we do not need to be told much about it (we already know, for example, that 'Bond' means James Bond, suave sophisticated handsome British spy) – with new information, on the other hand, we need to be told more. This means that given information tends to come in short noun phrases (often single words, or pronouns, for example, *Bond, he*), while new information comes in longer structures. Consequently, X elements are usually much longer (heavier) than S elements:

> S(Bond)   (stood and gazed out)   X(across the sparkling water barrier between Europe and Asia)

> S(he)   (turned back)   X(into the room, now bright with sunshine)

Joining clauses together

WITHOUT LINKS

It is rare to find a written text in English where the clauses are not linked in some way: absence of linkage produces a staccato, apparently crude style:

> It was raining. I picked up my coat. I put it on. I went to the door. I opened it. I went outside.

(Notice that even when texts have no linguistic links between clauses, we tend to organise them by time, putting clauses in the order in which they happened.)

COORDINATION

The simplest way to link clauses is by **coordination,** using words such as *and* or *but.* This type of linkage tends not to differentiate between the clauses joined – they appear to be equally important:

> It was raining but I picked up my coat and put it on. I went to the door and opened it. I went outside.

SUBORDINATION

A more complex way to link clauses is by **subordination.** Here, two clauses are linked in such a way that only one of them could stand on its own. This can be contrasted with coordination, where both clauses potentially retain their independence.

In subordination, one clause (the one which cannot be deleted) is the **main** clause, while the other (which often has a relationship of time, or cause and effect to the main clause) is the **subordinate** clause:

Because it was raining, I picked up my coat and put it on. I went to the door and after I opened it I went outside.

Note that the main clause is not deletable:

Because it was raining, I picked up my coat. →
*Because it was raining.

but the subordinate one is:

I picked up my coat.

Clauses are also often linked to noun phrases by subordination in order to supply more information about the head noun:

NP(The green figs SubClause (ready peeled)) VP(were bursting) X(with ripeness)

The subordinate nature of *ready peeled* here is shown by the fact that it is deletable.

The sentence

So far, we have talked about clauses rather than sentences. The reason for this is simple: sentences don't exist.

Definitions of the sentence (often along the lines of 'a single idea') just won't stand up to linguistic scrutiny – they aren't useful as a descriptive model. The only workable definition of a sentence is as something which begins with a capital letter and ends with a full stop – it only exists in written texts, and then only as an orthographical convention. What we call a clause – SV and optional X – may occupy the space between a capital and a full stop, or there may be two or more clauses present, or none (a surprising number of 'sentences' in novels are in fact made up solely of noun phrases). Writers can, and do, play around with the notion of the sentence.

3.2 Analysing clause structure

Definition

The best way to analyse clauses is to begin by finding the main verb (V): it is the one which can't be deleted. Then find the subject (S) – most frequently the noun phrase to the left of the main verb (again, this is not usually deletable). Within X, adverbial (Av) elements will often be deletable and mobile, while the object/complement (O/C) will not be deletable. Replacing large S or O/C elements with one word, and deleting Av elements, greatly simplifies analysis.

EXAMPLE

Here is a step-by-step analysis of the first sentence from Text 1 (we have deleted a parenthetic clause, 'she'd learned growing up in the dark', to simplify the analysis):

Wives were the ladies found tied to scuttled boats at the bottom of the lake, their hair embraced by the seaweed.

1   Find the main verb, which should not be deletable:

*Wives ... the ladies found tied to scuttled boats at the bottom of the lake, their hair embraced by the seaweed.

Wives *were* the ladies at the bottom of the lake, their hair embraced by the seaweed.

were can't be deleted.

2   Locate the subject, most likely to be to the left of the main verb. The main verb should agree with this in terms of person/number. Element to the left of the main verb:

S(*Wives*) V(*were*) ...

Check for agreement by changing number:

S(His wife)   V(*was*) ...

3   Locate X either by deletion, substitution, or movement:

*Wives were . . .

In this clause, although everything after *were* could swap places with *Wives*, it cannot be deleted. X is therefore mobile, but not deletable, and is therefore not an adverbial. We could replace the whole of this X element with the word *this*.

4   Analysis:

S(Wives) V(were) X(the ladies found tied to scuttled boats at the bottom of the lake, their hair embraced by the seaweed).

Note that the very large X element can be simplified here by replacing it with one word:

Wives were X(this).

Exercises

Analyse the following:

1   Cigarettes cause cancer.

2   Eagerly he tucked in.

3   She was suddenly angry.

Comment

1   S(Cigarettes) V(cause) X(cancer)

The subject can be identified by testing for person agreement on the verb:

S(Cigarettes) V(cause) cancer
S(Smoking) V(causes) cancer

2   X(Eagerly) S(he) V(tucked in)

X here is mobile and deletable, so it is an adverbial (Av):

> He tucked in X Av(eagerly).
> He tucked in.
> He X Av(eagerly) tucked in.

3   S(She)   V(was)   X Av(suddenly)   O/C(angry)

X here contains both Av and O/C – note that only Av is deletable:

> *She was suddenly
> She was angry

TASK

> Read Text 1.
>   Aside from the first, where there is a parenthetic clause 'she'd learned growing up in the dark' which you can ignore, every sentence has a similar grammatical structure. Identify it, and comment on its stylistic effect.

TEXT 1

Wives, she'd learned growing up in the dark, were the ladies found tied to scuttled boats at the bottom of the lake, their hair embraced by the seaweed. Husbands were men with their heads bashed in, doused with alcohol, stuck under the driver's wheel, and shoved over the cliff. Wives were tautly strung creatures you plotted against with optical illusions, tape recorders, coincidences, and evil servants until they went mad and you inherited the estate. Husbands were dull sofas you schemed against with your convertible boyfriends who knew how to talk him into increasing his insurance at the critical moment. Wives were victims pushed beyond endurance, then snatched suddenly back from the edge by that final straw we carry from birth just in time to butcher beer bellies in the bedroom. Husbands were worms that turned on the 'femmes fatales' who were too cocky to plot his death and got strangled with piano wire.

Solution

S(Wives) V(were) X(the ladies found tied to scuttled boats at the bottom of the lake, their hair embraced by the seaweed).

S(Husbands) V(were) X(men with their heads bashed in, doused with alcohol, stuck under the driver's wheel, and shoved over the cliff).

S(Wives) V(were) X(tautly strung creatures you plotted against with optical illusions, tape recorders, coincidences, and evil servants until they went mad and you inherited the estate).

S(Husbands) V(were) X(dull sofas you schemed against with your convertible boyfriends who knew how to talk him into increasing his insurance at the critical moment).

S(Wives) V(were) X(victims pushed beyond endurance, then snatched suddenly back from the edge by that final straw we carry from birth just in time to butcher beer bellies in the bedroom).

S(Husbands) V(were) X(worms that turned on the 'femmes fatales' who were too cocky to plot his death and got strangled with piano wire).

ATTRIBUTION

Toni Cade Bambara, 'The Survivor' from *Gorilla, My Love*, p. 100.

Verdict

Every sentence in this text has the structure SVX, where S is either *Husbands* or *Wives*, V is *were*, and X is a very long element. Therefore, the subjects and verbs in this text are very light in comparison to the X elements, consisting of just two words.

The repetitive pattern of 'plural noun + *be*' is the pattern of the aphorism or folk-wisdom (e.g. *all cats are grey in the night*, *roses are red*, *grass is green*, *the sky is blue*).

Using the aphoristic form with heavy X elements means that the passage shifts constantly from the very general to the very specific, but a specific which is presented as if it were the norm; as if every wife's life followed the pattern laid out here. Our expectations of the aphorism don't match with what we actually find, and we have to force ourselves to see these details as unusual. Compare the way this passage works with that by Nabokov in Section 1.4, which also assumes familiarity with certain genres of film.

3.3   The relationship between S and V

Definition

As a rule of thumb, S is the noun phrase to the left of the main verb; as a rule of semantics, S is the person who does the verb; as a rule of grammar, S and V have to agree for number and person:

S(Cigarettes)   V(cause)   cancer
S(Smoking)   V(causes)   cancer

Note that changing the number on the O/C element does not affect the verb:

Cigarettes   V(cause)   X O/C(cancers)
Cigarettes   V(cause)   X O/C(cancer)

Note that the rule of thumb about S appearing to the left of the verb does not always work. It is sometimes possible for writers to swap S and X in order to emphasise X:

X (Above them)   V(towers)   S(Jane Bowles, the weirdest writer of all)

Read through Text 2, which is the opening of a novel. What kind of atmosphere is created?

Can you explain this by the way the passage patterns SVX elements – their order, relative sizes, and the tense used on V?

Look also at the types of things that are placed in S position, and their relationship to V. How does this contribute to the effect?

TEXT 2

It is night-time, early evening. The lights of the house lie along a line. On the left is the kitchen. Below the pots of coriander on the windowsill stares the light bulb in a glass calyx shade. There is no one about. The clock in the stove tells the time but emits no sound. On two cooling racks three pale-yellow sponge cakes lie cooling. The curtains of the next window, partly drawn, leave a slice of light on the lawn. The light cuts into a table, massed with books: at the table, a girl in a dark gym tunic is seated, humped over, tongue crammed into cheek, writing. Her hair, which is greasy, stands on end, skewered into rough tufts around her left ear. Her right hand works at speed; she cannot keep her eyes off it. Her left lies flat on the page with the careful, balancing action of a child who first learns to form letters – as though she were pacifying the pace of the words. At moments when she looks up, this hand drifts back to her head, around the ear, there to work and twist.

At the far end of the house lies what must be the living-room. At all angles stand chairs, occupied by trim rotund cushions, lapped in brocade antimacassars. On the sofa, facing the open window, sits a woman. She is reading, though she has also been knitting. She gets up and walks over to the piano. Momentarily, her hand lies spread over the keys. She looks down at the keyboard, but thinks better of it. She walks back to the sofa, picks up the magazine. She fumbles with an attached perfume sample; the sachet will not come open. She sits down. She reaches for the portable radio at her side. Her thumb and forefinger are pursed around the on/off knob, but she thinks better of it. She settles back in the sofa. There is no sound about. The TV is flickering.

It is midnight. There are two lights on in the house. One is on in a bedroom. Two beds stand in close parallel, separated by a bedside table; only one bed is turned down. On the bedside table, painted buff eggshell off-white, lies a New English Bible, abutting on a colonnade of pill phials. On the bed are spread a long nightshirt and pyjama trousers, the elastic slacked into bagginess. There is no one about. The young girl must be asleep because in the other lit window, elongated like a Cranach figure by the effect of framing, the woman is visible. She is standing at the table where the girl was working. As with the girl, the woman's head is bent over the books. The sickle of chin brackets that of nose. She moves her hands in amongst the books, stops herself, moves the books again. She spends some time in this manner, shuffling, pausing, shuffling, then retreats to the bedroom empty-handed. She does not forget to turn off the light.

ATTRIBUTION

Elleke Boehmer, *Screens against the Sky*, pp. 3–4.

Solution

The dominant clause structure here is SVX. It is also the case that many clauses conform to our expectations about the relative sizes of S and X elements (see 3.4), for example in the first sentence:

S(It)   V(is)   X(night-time, early evening)

However, the basic pattern is varied – in the second sentence, for example, S is **heavier** (larger) than X:

S(The lights of the house)   V(lie)   X(along a line)

while in the third sentence, X is placed at the front of the clause:

X(On the left)   V(is)   S(the kitchen)

and in the fourth sentence this type of construction is repeated, with the slots before and after the verb both expanded:

X(Below the pots of coriander on the windowsill)
V(stares)   S(the light bulb in a glass calyx shade)

The fifth sentence mirrors the structure of the first:

S(There)   V(is)   X(no one about)

Note too that the passage uses the simple present tense – relatively unusual in novels (see 2.4).

We can say, therefore, that these clauses have a simple basic structure – they are almost all SVX with V in the present tense – but that Boehmer varies the structure. On the one hand the pattern is not so insistent that it calls attention to itself; on the other the variations are not so great that they disrupt the repetitive effect. This structural patterning, and the use of present tense, gives the passage its sense of inevitability – things could not be other than as they are (note the high frequency of the verb *be*).

When the types of thing that fill the subject role are analysed, it becomes clear that human agency is almost entirely lacking from the piece:

It, The lights, the kitchen, the light bulb, There, The clock, cakes, The curtains, The light

Despite the semantic rule that the subject 'does' the verb, and is therefore likely to be an animate being, here subjects are often inanimate objects and dummy subjects (*It* and *there*). This subverts our expectations of the relationship between the subject and verb. Note too that the first human subject element, *a girl*, is the subject of a passive verb, *is seated* (see 2.5). This absence of human action is continued – parts of the girl, rather than she herself, are the subjects of subsequent verbs: her hair stands, her right hand writes, even her eyes behave independently. In the second paragraph, the woman begins three actions, but breaks off each one: she almost plays the piano, almost opens some perfume, almost turns the radio on or off.

The combined effect of this is of distance – the narrator appears not to be familiar with the house, yet describes it in great detail. There is a lot of restless activity going on, but it is disconnected: the woman does not complete her actions; only parts of the girl act, rather than her as an entity.

3.4   Relative size of syntactic elements: light X elements

Definition

In English clauses, the commonest order of syntactic elements is S (subject) V (verb) X (object, complement and/or adverbial). This is the normal word order in English.

In most clauses the first-mentioned element (S) will usually have been mentioned before in a previous clause. It is therefore 'given' information. In contrast, the X element will usually contain 'new' information – either extra information about S, or a completely new person, thing or topic.

```
S    V       X           S   V    X
He   walked  the dog.    It  was  a cute little chihuahua
given        new         given    new . . .
```

Because the given information has, by definition, already been mentioned, it can often appear as a pronoun (as in the examples above). In contrast, because new information is being presented for the first time, the element containing it tends to be large (or 'heavy').

These tendencies mean that S elements are usually lighter than X elements in English clauses – and writers can fulfil or thwart our expectations of clause element order and relative size for effect.

EXAMPLES

```
S V    X
I was  a student at the University of Wisconsin
given  new . . .
```

```
S          V          X
Humboldt   revealed   to me new ways of doing things
given                 new . . .


S     V     X
He    was   a pioneer
given       new . . .
```

Identify the SVX elements in the following:

1   I read Harlequin Ballads enthusiastically.

2   He gave me black coffee.

3   The book of ballads published by Von Humboldt Fleisher in the thirties
     was an immediate hit.

(3) follows the SVX pattern, with everything up to the verb (*was*) forming
the subject:

> S(The book of ballads published by Von Humboldt Fleisher in the
> thirties) V(was) X(an immediate hit)

Compare:

> S(It) was an immediate hit

This is because everything between *book* and *was* postmodifies *book*. So
although this sentence has an unusually heavy subject, it is still following
the SVX pattern.

TASK

TASK 1

Get someone to read Text 3 aloud to you – can you hear any patterns?
Identify the S and X elements in this text and compare their relative size.
How does this conform to normal expectations?

TASK 2

Now do the same for Text 4, and compare your findings.

TEXT 3

The book of ballads published by Von Humboldt Fleisher in the thirties was an immediate hit. Humboldt was just what everyone had been waiting for. Out in the Midwest I had certainly been waiting eagerly, I can tell you that. An avant-garde writer, the first of a new generation, he was handsome, fair, large, serious, witty, he was learned. The guy had it all. All the papers reviewed his book. His picture appeared in Time without insult and in Newsweek with praise. I read Harlequin Ballads enthusiastically. I was a student at the University of Wisconsin and thought about nothing but literature day and night. Humboldt revealed to me new ways of doing things. I was ecstatic. I envied his luck, his talent, and his fame, and I went east in May to have a look at him – perhaps to get next to him. The Greyhound bus, taking the Scranton route, made the trip in about fifty hours. That didn't matter. The bus windows were open. I had never seen real mountains before. Trees were budding. It was like Beethoven's Pastorale. I felt showered by the green, within. Manhattan was fine, too. I took a room for three bucks a week and found a job selling Fuller Brushes door to door. And I was wildly excited about everything. Having written Humboldt a long fan letter, I was invited to Greenwich Village to discuss literature and ideas. He lived on Bedford Street, near Chumley's. First he gave me black coffee, and then poured gin in the same cup. 'Well, you're a nice-looking enough fellow, Charlie,' he said to me. 'Aren't you a bit sly, maybe? I think you're headed for early baldness. And such large emotional handsome eyes. But you certainly do love literature and that's the main thing. You have sensibility,' he said. He was a pioneer in the use of this word. Sensibility later made it big. Humboldt was very kind. He introduced me to people in the Village and got me books to review. I always loved him.

TEXT 4

A junior associate of the old Partisan Review gang, Harold Stone had become known as a wunderkind even before he came down from Harvard with an essay titled 'Bakunin and the Idea of an Avant-Garde.' He took a job at Knopf, shared a girl with Bellow and got his glasses broken by Mailer, thereby sealing his reputation. At increasing intervals, he published essays and book reviews that were much discussed in the closing days of the last literary establishment in New York. Along the way he had married a young Waspy debutante who now led an entirely separate existence in New Canaan, Connecticut, though they remained married. Fresh from the suburban Midwest, Russell had devoured Harold's editions of Sartre and Camus and Gramsci in college; he had read Harold's essays on Lukacs and Kafka. When he arrived in Manhattan after graduate work at Oxford, Russell had been fortunate to find a job at the venerable publishing house where Harold reigned, and to come to the older man's attention by way of some poems he had had published in a quarterly. Perhaps Harold had felt nostalgic for the idea of literary young men coming to the city, grateful for the idea that young men were still writing poetry at all, in the manner of his friends from the Village days so long past; curious to know what the smart young men were reading nowadays; guilty possibly, because as likely as not he was about to have lunch at The Four Seasons with a millionaire author of espionage thrillers. At any rate, Harold had seen something in the poems. He first took Russell out to lunch and later took him under his prickly, owlish wing.

Solution

Note: ( ) indicates ellipsis.

TEXT 3

1 S(The book of ballads published by Von Humboldt Fleisher in the thirties) V(was) X(an immediate hit.)
2 S(Humboldt) V(was) X(just what everyone had been waiting for.)
3 X(Out in the Midwest) S(I) V(had certainly been waiting) X(eagerly,) S(I) V(can tell) X(you that.)
4 S(An avant-garde writer, the first of a new generation, he) V(was) X(handsome, fair, large, serious, witty,) S(he) V(was) X(learned.)
5 S(The guy) V(had) X(it all.)
6 S(All the papers) V(reviewed) X(his book.)
7 S(His picture) V(appeared) X(in Time without insult and in Newsweek with praise.)
8 S(I) V(read) X(Harlequin Ballads enthusiastically.)
9 S(I) V(was) X(a student at the University of Wisconsin) and S( ) V(thought about) X(nothing but literature day and night.)
10 S(Humboldt) V(revealed) X(to me new ways of doing things.)
11 S(I) V(was) X(ecstatic.)
12 S(I) V(envied) X(his luck, his talent, and his fame,) and S(I) V(went) X(east in May to have a look at him – perhaps to get next to him.)
13 S(The Greyhound bus, taking the Scranton route,) V(made) X(the trip in about fifty hours.)
14 S(That) V(didn't matter.)
15 S(The bus windows) V(were) X(open.)
16 S(I) V(had never seen) X(real mountains before.)
17 S(Trees) V(were budding.)
18 S(It) V(was) X(like Beethoven's Pastorale.)
19 S(I) V(felt showered) X(by the green, within.)

20   S(Manhattan) V(was) X(fine, too.)
21   S(I) V(took) X(a room for three bucks a week) and S( ) V(found) X(a job selling Fuller Brushes door to door.)
22   And S(I) V(was wildly excited) X(about everything.)
23   X(Having written Humboldt a long fan letter,) S(I) V(was invited) X(to Greenwich Village to discuss literature and ideas.)
24   S(He) V(lived) X(on Bedford Street, near Chumley's.)
25   X(First) S(he) V(gave) X(me black coffee,) and X(then) S( ) V(poured) X(gin in the same cup.)
26   X('Well,) S(you) V('re) X(a nice-looking enough fellow, Charlie,') S(he) V(said) X(to me.)
27   V('Aren't) S(you) X(a bit sly, maybe?)
28   S(I) V(think) X(you're headed for early baldness.)
29   And S( ) V( ) X(such large emotional handsome eyes.)
     [*i.e. 'You have such large emotional handsome eyes'*]
30   But S(you) X(certainly) V(do love) X(literature) and S(that) V('s) X(the main thing.)
31   S(You) V(have) X(sensibility,') S(he) V(said.)
32   S(He) V(was) X(a pioneer in the use of this word.)
33   S(Sensibility) X(later) V(made) X(it big.)
34   S(Humboldt) V(was) X(very kind.)
35   S(He) V(introduced) X(me to people in the Village) and S( ) V(got) X(me books to review.)
36   S(I) X(always) V(loved) X(him.)

TEXT 4

1   S(A junior associate of the old Partisan Review gang, Harold Stone) V(had become known as) X(a wunderkind even before he came down from Harvard with an essay titled 'Bakunin and the Idea of an Avant-Garde.')
2   S(He) V(took) X(a job at Knopf,) S( ) V(shared) X(a girl with Bellow) and S( ) V(got) X(his glasses broken by Mailer, thereby sealing his reputation.)
3   X(At increasing intervals,) S(he) V(published) X(essays and book reviews that were much discussed in the closing days of the last literary establishment in New York.)
4   X(Along the way) S(he) V(had married) X(a young Waspy debutante

who now led an entirely separate existence in New Canaan, Connecticut, though they remained married.)

5   X(Fresh from the suburban Midwest,) S(Russell) V(had devoured) X(Harold's editions of Sartre and Camus and Gramsci in college;) S(he) V(had read) X(Harold's essays on Lukacs and Kafka.)

6   X(When he arrived in Manhattan after graduate work at Oxford,) S(Russell) V(had been) X(fortunate to find a job at the venerable publishing house where Harold reigned, and to come to the older man's attention by way of some poems he had had published in a quarterly.)

7   X(Perhaps) S(Harold) V(had felt) X(nostalgic for the idea of literary young men coming to the city, grateful for the idea that young men were still writing poetry at all, in the manner of his friends from the Village days so long past; curious to know what the smart young men were reading nowadays; guilty possibly, because as likely as not he was about to have lunch at The Four Seasons with a millionaire author of espionage thrillers.)

8   X(At any rate,) S(Harold) V(had seen) X(something in the poems.)

9   S(He) X(first) V(took) X(Russell out to lunch) and X(later) V(took) X(him under his prickly, owlish wing.)

ATTRIBUTION

Text 3   Saul Bellow, *Humboldt's Gift*, p. 5.
Text 4   Jay McInerney, *Brightness Falls*, p. 34.

Verdict

Text 3, by and large, follows the unmarked pattern for the order of elements (that is, SVX). However, many of the X elements are extremely light. This happens especially between sentences (14)–(20) ('That didn't matter' to 'Manhattan was fine, too'). Notice how many sentences are single-clause sentences. Such SVX ordering, with very light X elements, can give the impression of writing for very young children, that is:

Janet saw Spot. Spot is a dog. Spot wagged his tail.

but is not found frequently in adult literature. Rather, in adult literature, we expect to find a whole range of pre- or postmodifying subordinate clauses in the X element.

This is the opening passage of the novel, so we cannot determine whether the narrator, a fledgeling author, is as yet unsophisticated in literary technique (and his style will develop through the novel as he matures) or whether he is trying to be 'avant-garde' like Humboldt, and thinks this somewhat *faux-naïf* style might be the way to do it.

Text 4, even though it is dealing with a very similar topic, has much larger X elements. We could, if we wanted, further break down most of these X elements into SVX structure, since most contain subordinate clauses, for example:

4 X(a young Waspy debutante (S(who) X(now) V(led) X(an entirely separate existence in New Canaan, Connecticut), (though S(they) V(remained married))))

Use of subordination like this to expand X elements is the normal, unmarked practice in most fiction: although Bellow's style is syntactically less complex, it is the less usual – and more original – one.

3.5   Obligatory X elements (transitivity)

Definition

We have defined clause structure in English as SV(X) where the X element is optional. However, certain verbs require an X element to be present for their clause to be grammatical – these are termed transitive verbs:

    She   tested   the wiring.
    S   V   X

but not:

    *She   tested.
    S   V

Other verbs do not require an X element – these are termed intransitive:

They   walked.
S   V

He   wrote.
S   V

Verbs which can be used intransitively (without X) can also often be used transitively:

They   walked   along the cliff.
S   V   X

He   wrote   *War and Peace.*
S   V   X

Purely transitive verbs are much less likely to be used intransitively, for example:

*He put.

TASK

Read through Text 5.
    Identify the verbs and comment on whether they are purely transitive, or are verbs which can be used with or without X (try deleting X).
    Do you find anything unusual in the pattern of transitivity in the text?

Through the fence, between the curling flower spaces, I could see them hitting. They were coming toward where the flag was and I went along the fence. Luster was hunting in the grass by the flower tree. They took the flag out, and they were hitting. Then they put the flag back and they went to the table, and he hit and the other hit. Then they went on, and I went along the fence. Luster came away from the flower tree and we went along the fence and they stopped and we stopped and I looked through the fence while Luster was hunting in the grass.

'Here, caddie.' He hit. They went away across the pasture. I held to the fence and watched them going away.

'Listen at you, now,' Luster said. 'Ain't you something, thirty-three years old, going on that way. After I done went all the way to town to buy you that cake. Hush up that moaning. Ain't you going to help me find that quarter so I can go to the show tonight.'

They were hitting little, across the pasture. I went back along the fence to where the flag was. It flapped on the bright grass and the trees.

Solution

Transitive verbs (X must be present):

```
I   could see   them   hitting   [?]
            S      V       X

They  took  the flag out  and  they  were hitting  [?]
S     V     X                  S     V             X
they  put   the flag back
S     V     X
he    hit   [?]  and  the other  hit  [?]
S     V     X         S          V    X
```

```
He   hit   [?]
S    V     X
find   that quarter
V      X
```

ATTRIBUTION

William Faulkner, *The Sound and the Fury*, p. 11.

Verdict

Most of the transitive verbs in this passage are used normally, with X elements – *to take, to put, to find*. *To hit*, however, is consistently used intransitively, without X, although this violates our expectations of the way this verb should behave. We expect to see something like *they were hitting the ball*, or *they were hitting it lightly*, or even *they were hitting the ball with small strokes*.

Gradually it becomes clear that this is a description of a golf-match. 'Between the curling flower spaces' can be interpreted as looking between the blossoms of a tree in flower. 'Hitting little' can be interpreted as putting. That the narrator is more than just a person unfamiliar with golf is made clear by the unexpected grammar – this hints at a clinical problem, rather than simple puzzlement. In fact the narrator of this passage is mentally retarded.

3.6   Expansion of X elements

Definition

The default word order in present-day English is SVX where S stands for subject, V for verb, and X for object, complement or adverbial. Although many utterances do not follow this pattern, we can say that SVX is the unmarked pattern in present-day English.

1   S(He)   V(looked)   X(down)
2   S(He)   V(clicked)   X(his light out)
3   S(He)   V(found)   X(there was just enough filtering through the mist which hung eighteen foot up and which did not descend to the ground, to make out Ted, his goose, about already, a dirty pallor, almost the same colour as Alice, the Persian cat, that kept herself dry where every blade of grass bore its dark, mist laden string of water)

Exercises

Identify the SVX elements in the following:

1   He saw plain how Ted was not ringed in by fog.

2   The goose posed staring, head to one side.

Comment

As example (3) shows, it is possible for the X element to be very heavy. This is in accord with the unmarked pattern for information in English sentences (**given** first, **new** last) which tends to ensure that things we know least about, and therefore want most information on, come last – the unmarked tendency (certainly in spoken English) is therefore for S and V to be relatively light, and X to be relatively heavy.

TASK

Analyse the SVX distribution in Text 6.

TEXT 6

He looked down. He clicked his light out. He found there was just enough filtering through the mist which hung eighteen foot up and which did not descend to the ground, to make out Ted, his goose, about already, a dirty pallor, almost the same colour as Alice, the Persian cat, that kept herself dry where every blade of grass bore its dark, mist laden string of water.

—Old and deaf, half blind, Mr Rock said about himself, the air raw in his throat. Nevertheless he saw plain how Ted was not ringed in by fog. For the goose posed staring, head to one side, with a single eye, straight past the house, up into the fog bank which had made all daylight deaf beneath, and beyond which, at some clear height, Mr Rock knew now there must be a flight of birds fast winging,

—Ted knows where, he thought.

Solution

1   S(He)   V(looked)   X(down.)

2   S(He)   V(clicked)   X(his light out.)

3   S(He)   V(found)   X(there was just enough filtering through the mist which hung eighteen foot up and which did not descend to the ground, to make out Ted, his goose, about already, a dirty pallor, almost the same colour as Alice, the Persian cat, that kept herself dry where every blade of grass bore its dark, mist laden string of water.)

4   (S( ) V( )) X(—Old and deaf, half blind,) S(Mr Rock) V(said) X(about himself, the air raw in his throat.)

5   X(Nevertheless) S(he) V(saw) X(plain how Ted was not ringed in by fog.)

6   For S(the goose) V(posed) X(staring, head to one side, with a single eye, straight past the house, up into the fog bank which had made all daylight deaf beneath, and beyond which, at some clear height, Mr Rock knew now there must be a flight of birds fast winging,)

7   S(—Ted) V(knows) X(where,) S(he) V(thought.)

ATTRIBUTION

Henry Green, *Concluding*, p. 5.

Verdict

This passage begins with two simple sentences, but is dominated by two long, multiply subordinate sentences:

> S(He) V(found) X(there was just enough filtering through the mist which hung eighteen foot up and which did not descend to the ground, to make out Ted, his goose, about already, a dirty pallor, almost the same colour as Alice, the Persian cat, that kept herself dry where every blade of grass bore its dark, mist laden string of water.)

> S(the goose) V(posed) X(staring, head to one side, with a single eye, straight past the house, up into the fog bank which had made all daylight deaf beneath, and beyond which, at some clear height, Mr Rock knew now there must be a flight of birds fast winging,)

Each of these sentences consists of light S and V elements with a very heavy X element indeed. In both cases, most of the expansion of the X element consists of post-head modification (slot 4), sometimes of more than one noun phrase:

mist	which hung eighteen foot up
	which did not descend to the ground
Ted	his goose
	about already
	a dirty pallor
Alice	the Persian cat
	that kept herself dry.

Again in both cases, Green disrupts our expectations of subordination and post-head modification by the introduction of new subjects which are themselves taken up as the main topic, rather than serving to illustrate the first mentioned noun phrase – thus we move from fog to Ted to Alice, without the expected return to the fog, or Ted.

Very involved post-head modification like this, especially when it apparently forgets the main topic, can be seen as mimicking speech – so that the language of the passage thus becomes iconic of the process of Mr Rock's perception of events, and his self-narration of them. Although based on the unmarked structures of speech, these sentences are very extreme examples of heavy X elements (try reading them aloud), and may also serve to mimic the old man's rambling thought processes.

Because the X elements are so heavy, the reader may have to reread this text more than once in order to process it. Notice how this is what the old man is doing: he's peering down through the fog, looking at his cat and goose. The fog has muffled the light and sound, and so deprived him of his ability to process information received by his senses. He has to work to make out Ted and Alice, and is unable to make out the flock of birds at all.

3.7   Heavy S and X elements before the verb

Definition

The commonest order of syntactic elements in English clauses is SVX (subject plus verb, then an object and/or complement and/or an adverbial). This is the normal word order in English.

In texts, the initial (S) element of a clause will generally have been mentioned before in a previous clause. It is therefore termed *given* information. In contrast, the X element will usually contain *new* information – either extra information about S, or a completely new person, thing or topic.

```
S        V          X
(He)     (walked)   (the dog)
given               new

S        V        X
(It)     (was)    (a cute little chihuahua)
given             new
```

Because the given information has, by definition, already been mentioned, it can often appear as a pronoun (as in the example above). In contrast, because new information is being presented for the first time, the element containing it tends to be large (or 'heavy').

These tendencies mean that S elements are usually lighter than X elements in English clauses – and writers can fulfil or thwart our expectations of clause element order and relative size for effect.

S   V   X
(He)   (reached)   (the hotel)

S   V   X
(They)   (would dine)   (together at the worst)

Exercises

Identify by deletion and substitution the preverbal S and X elements in the following:

1   The principle I have just mentioned as operating had been, with the most newly disembarked of the two ment, wholly destructive.
2   A telegram from him bespeaking a room 'only if not noisy', reply paid, was produced.

Comment

The preverbal S elements are:

1   (The principle I have just mentioned as operating) had been . . .
     for example: (It) had been . . .

2   (A telegram from him bespeaking a room 'only if not noisy', reply paid,) was produced.
     for example: (It) was produced.

The default clause structure in English is SVX, with S lighter than X. In both of these sentences the S element is either heavier than X, or almost as heavy.

TASK

Identify the preverbal S and X elements in the following text.
What effects do they create?

TEXT 7

Strether's first question, when he reached the hotel, was about his friend; yet on his learning that Waymarsh was apparently not to arrive till evening he was not wholly disconcerted. A telegram from him bespeaking a room 'only if not noisy', reply paid, was produced for the inquirer at the office, so that the understanding they should meet at Chester rather than at Liverpool remained to that extent sound. The same secret principle, however, that had prompted Strether not absolutely to desire Waymarsh's presence at the dock, that had led him thus to postpone for a few hours his enjoyment of it, now operated to make him feel he could still wait without disappointment. They would dine together at the worst, and with all respect to dear old Waymarsh – if not even, for that matter, to himself – there was little fear that in the sequel they shouldn't see enough of each other. The principle I have just mentioned as operating had been, with the most newly disembarked of the two men, wholly instinctive – the fruit of a sharp sense that, delightful as it would be to find himself looking, after so much separation, into his comrade's face, his business would be a trifle bungled should he simply arrange for this countenance to present itself to the nearing steamer as the first 'note' of Europe. Mixed with everything was the apprehension, already, on Strether's part, that he would, at best, throughout, prove the note of Europe in quite a sufficient degree.

Solution

1   S(Strether's first question,) X(when he reached the hotel,) V(was) X(about his friend;) X(yet on his learning that Waymarsh was apparently not to arrive till evening) S(he) V(was not wholly disconcerted.)

2   S(A telegram from him bespeaking a room 'only if not noisy', reply paid,) V(was produced) X(for the inquirer at the office,) so that S(the understanding they should meet at Chester rather than at Liverpool) V(remained) X(to that extent sound.)

3   S(The same secret principle, however, that had prompted Strether not absolutely to desire Waymarsh's presence at the dock, that had led him thus to postpone for a few hours his enjoyment of it,) X(now) V(operated) X(to make him feel he could still wait without disappointment.)

4   S(They) V(would dine) X(together at the worst,) and X(with all respect to dear old Waymarsh – if not even, for that matter, to himself –) S(there) V(was) X(little fear that in the sequel they shouldn't see enough of each other.)

5   S(The principle I have just mentioned as operating) V(had been,) X(with the most newly disembarked of the two men, wholly instinctive – the fruit of a sharp sense that, delightful as it would be to find himself looking, after so much separation, into his comrade's face, his business would be a trifle bungled should he simply arrange for this countenance to present itself to the nearing steamer as the first 'note' of Europe.)

6   X(Mixed with everything) V(was) S(the apprehension, already, on Strether's part, that he would, at best, throughout, prove the note of Europe in quite a sufficient degree.)

ATTRIBUTION

Henry James, *The Ambassadors*, p. 5.

Verdict

The main syntactic feature of this text is a succession of very heavy preverbal elements. This is a marked characteristic, as the preverbal elements in English are usually light. It gives the text its dense, difficult-to-follow quality. This is because our normal processing expectations are constantly upset by the delaying of the main verb (V); and sometimes we are misled by the presence of a subordinate verb before the main one. The frequent heavy modification of S elements and the constant interpolation of X elements helps to give the impression of a punctilious, even rather pedantic, central character, who is perhaps made acutely self-aware by being in a foreign country.

The other effect of the delaying of the main verb is to echo the delights of postponement so dwelt upon in the passage. Strether savours and wants to extend the time before he has to meet his old friend, and expresses this apparent paradox by means of negativisation as well as preverbal modification. Notice the number and position of negatives in the text. Not only is the word *not* repeated, but there are also words and phrases such as *not wholly disconcerted*, *without disappointment*, *at the worst*, *a trifle bungled*, *apprehension*, which whilst acting as positive in context, are constituted of negative elements. These two syntactic techniques show Strether's contrary state of mind – he both wants to meet his old friend, and also to put off the moment as long as possible.

Note: This passage has been considered in some detail by Ian Watt in his essay, 'The First Paragraph of James's *Ambassadors*', *Essays in Criticism*, X (1960), pp. 250–74.

3.8   Placement of adverbials in the clause

Definition

In the introduction (3.1), we established that SVX is the normal clause structure for English. We also said that X could consist of either O/C (object or complement) or Av (adverbial element), or both, but that it was not always necessary to distinguish them.

In this section, we do want to distinguish these elements, and it is possible to do this by looking at the way O/C and Av behave in clauses.

Normally, it will be possible to move adverbial elements around in the clause much more easily than O/C:

```
I    read the letter    at once
S  V    O/C             Av
```

```
I   at once   read   the letter
S   Av        V      O/C

At once   I   read   the letter
Av        S   V      O/C
```

This mobility has to do with the fact that adverbial elements tend to carry additional information, rather than the crucial information carried by S, V or O/C. For this reason, it is also often possible to delete adverbial elements without making the clause ungrammatical:

I read the letter.

Typically, adverbial elements answer questions about the manner in which something was done, or why it was done:

When did you read the letter? *At once.*

Adverbial elements can be either single words:

I read the letter *immediately.*

or phrases:

At once, I read the letter.

or subordinate clauses:

I read the letter *as soon as I got it.*

Although the adverbial element is highly mobile in the clause, it is more likely to appear in some positions than others:

Likely: Bond ate his breakfast *at the table*
              At the table, Bond ate his breakfast
Less likely: Bond, *at the table*, ate his breakfast
              Bond ate, *at the table*, his breakfast

Placing adverbial elements in unexpected positions shifts the focus of a clause – either on to the adverbial element, or away from some other element. Note how in the following, emphasis is shifted on to two adverbial elements, 'with a travelling bag', and the final 'again' by their unusual positioning:

> Yet I had been home, for I was dressed in a winter coat and with a travelling bag I arrived in Euston Station. I was ashamed to be again in London.
>
> (Thomas Healy, *Rolling*, 1992, p. 114)

TASK

Read Text 8.
   Identify the adverbial elements and note any which seem to be out of their normal position.
   Account for their effect – are there any other aspects of the text which contribute to this?

TEXT 8

Hale knew, before he had been in Brighton three hours, that they meant to murder him. With his inky fingers and his bitten nails, his manner cynical and nervous, anybody could tell he didn't belong – belong to the early summer sun, the cool Whitsun wind off the sea, the holiday crowd. They came in by train from Victoria every five minutes, rocked down Queen's Road standing on the tops of the little local trams, stepped off in bewildered multitudes into fresh and glittering air: the new silver paint sparkled on the piers, the cream houses ran away into the west like a pale Victorian watercolour; a race in miniature motors, a band playing, flower gardens in bloom below the front, an aeroplane advertising something for the health in pale vanishing clouds across the sky.

   It had seemed quite easy to Hale to be lost in Brighton. Fifty thousand people besides himself were down for the day, and for quite a while he gave himself up to the good day, drinking gins and tonics wherever his programme allowed. For he had to stick closely to a programme: from ten till eleven Queen's Road and Castle Square, from eleven till twelve the Aquarium and Palace Pier, twelve till one the front between the Old Ship and West Pier, back for lunch between one and two in any restaurant he chose round the Castle Square, and after that he had to make his way all down the parade to the West Pier and then to the station by the Hove streets. These were the limits of his absurd and widely advertised sentry-go.

Advertised on every Messenger poster: 'Kolley Kibber in Brighton today.' In his pocket he had a packet of cards to distribute in hidden places along his route; those who found them would receive ten shillings from the Messenger, but the big prize was reserved for whoever challenged Hale with the proper form of words and with a copy of the Messenger in his hand: 'You are Mr Kolley Kibber. I claim the Daily Messenger prize.'

Verdict

These are the opening three paragraphs of Graham Greene's *Brighton Rock*. The first sentence in particular has been celebrated as one of the most striking in twentieth-century English novels. A great deal of its effect is due to Greene's placing of the time adverbial 'before he had been in Brighton three hours' in the least likely clause slot. It would be much more usual for this to have been placed at the end or start of the clause:

> Before he had been in Brighton three hours, Hale knew that they meant to murder him.

> Hale knew that they meant to murder him before he had been in Brighton three hours.

The effect of the shift is to imply that what is important is not that 'they' are about to murder Hale, but the time it takes him to realise this, and the location in Brighton. This is disconcerting for the reader. Notice that Greene deliberately uses other techniques to disorientate the reader: 'they' are never identified, contrary to our expectations of cohesive pronoun replacement; and instead of revealing why Hale is to be killed, or how he came to know this, we have a very matter-of-fact (because it is internally cohesive and coherent, and fulfils our expectations of adverbial placement) account of his duties in Brighton. This account ought to provide us with the information the first sentence deliberately withholds – but it does not.

Note further that there are in fact two bodies of people referred to as 'they' in the text – the people about to kill Hale, and the holiday crowds – and that the first mention of the second group of people is deliberately ambiguous, with 'they' placed in the S slot, normally reserved for given information. This invites us, at least temporarily, to confuse the two.

Just as the passage is about a paradox – a man in hiding following a public programme – so its structure is contradictory. It is apparently cohesive and coherent, and yet it does not explain the most important things: who Hale is; who 'they' are; how he knows they mean to kill him; why they would want to. By manipulating our expectations of informational structure Greene deliberately highlights questions he has no intention of answering, creating tension and suspense.

3.9 Main clauses

Definition

Subordination links two or more clauses in such a way that only one of them could stand alone. This clause is the main clause, and any others are subordinate to it. Main and subordinate clauses can usually be distinguished by deletion, for example:

Because it was raining, I picked up my coat.

There are two clauses here (*Because it was raining*, and *I picked up my coat*), but only one of them could stand alone:

*Because it was raining.
I picked up my coat.

I picked up my coat is thus the main clause.

In some cases, clauses which are subordinate could stand alone in different contexts. For example:

She hummed tune band was now playing.

contains two clauses (*She hummed tune* and *band was now playing*). It is possible to imagine a text in which (*The*) *band was now playing* would be a main clause, but note here that this clause functions to add information to *tune* – if we deleted *She hummed tune*, the sense of the sentence would change completely. If, on the other hand, we delete *band was now playing*, the sense of the sentence does not change.

Subordination contrasts with coordination, where clauses are joined on a basis of equal importance (coordination often uses words such as *and*, *but*, *or*), for example:

She clapped hands and clapped.

There are two clauses here: *She clapped hands* and (*She*) *clapped*. As is often the case with coordination, the pronoun subject (*She*) is not repeated in the second clause, but as long as this is supplied, the second clause could stand alone. This is not the case with **Because it was raining* above.

Comment

It is the norm for authors to use a variety of clause structures, that is, to use both main and subordinate clauses in a text and to vary between coordination and subordination. If only main clauses are used, there is a danger that the text will sound staccato or childish. If only sentences with many subordinate clauses are used, the text will run the risk of sounding too complicated and difficult to process.

TASK

What kind of clause structures do Texts 9 and 10 have?
Why do you think this might be?

They were in cinema. Band played tune tum tum did dee dee. She hugged Dale's arm. She jumped her knees to the time.

Couple on screen danced in ballroom there. She did not see them. Dee dee did da.

Tum tum tum tum tum. Dale did not budge. Dee dee de did dee. She hummed now. She rolled his arm between her palms. Da da did dee – did dee dee tum, ta.

'I do love this tune' she said.

'Ah' he said.

Did dee dee tum ta. Tune was over. She clapped hands and clapped. Applause was general. But film did not stop there oh no heroine's knickers slipped down slinky legs in full floor.

eeeee Lily Gates screamed.

OOEEE the audience.

And band took encore then. Tum tum ti tumpy tum.

Lily arranged her hair. Dum dum di dumpy dum. She hummed then.

She moved her knees in time. Heroine's father struggled with policeman now in full ballroom. She did not watch but jumped her knees now. Da da did DEE – (what a pause!) – did dee dee tum ta. Great clapping of hands. Attendant moved up gangway and shouted 'Order please.' He moved down. Lily Gates said to young Mr Dale he didn't take much interest in nothing did he? 'Why not take a bit of fun Jim when it comes your way?' she softly said. He said 'I can't enjoy this music when I'm not in the mood.' 'Why you funny' she said "ave a mood then.' He said 'Don't call me your names Lil when there's so many can 'ear you.'

'Why they're all listenin' to the music.' She was whispering 'Jim!'

She hummed tune band was now playing whey widdle o.

'It's 'ot in 'ere' he said.

'H O T warm' she said.

'Why they're playin' it again' she said. She looked at screen. She saw heroine's knickers again were coming down, now in young man's bed-room.

ooeee she screamed.

EEEEE the audience.

The band played that tune. Tum tum ti tumpy tum. Dum dum di dumpy dum. She jumped her knees to time. Da da DID DEE – (it wasn't her knickers after all) – did dee dee tum ta.

TEXT 10

The word 'Prologue' danced before her eyes, and Gracie felt in her stomach the sinking sensation that preceded dental work. She looked steadfastly at the clumsy covered wagons creeping across the plain and she gasped as there was a sudden close-up of herself, acting, in the canvas oval at a wagon's back.

LET US NEVER FORGET THE NOBLE MEN AND
WOMEN WHOSE SUPREME SACRIFICE MADE
POSSIBLE OUR GLORIOUS CITY

There were the Indians in the distance now – it was much more exciting that it had been on the suburban lot. The battle, looking desperately real, was in full swing. She sought herself anxiously amid the heat of conflict, but she might have been any one of a score of girls who it seemed had been acting just as violently as herself. And here was the climax already. A savage rode up threateningly. Bang! And Gracie, or someone who looked like Gracie, sank wounded to the ground.

'See that? See that?' she whispered excitedly to her father. 'That was hard to do, let me tell you!'

Someone said 'Sh!' and Gracie's eyes again sought the screen. The Indians were driven off, a hearty prayer was said by all, and the fields were expeditiously plowed for corn. Then, to Gracie's astonishment, the whole scene began to change. The suburban plain disappeared, and one of the covered wagons faded before her eyes into a handsome limousine. From the limousine stepped out a modern young girl in a fur coat with hat to match. It was none other than Miss Virginia Blue Ribbon, the pretty daughter of the owner of the Blue Ribbon store. Gracie stared. Was the pioneer part over, she wondered – in less than fifteen minutes? And what did this limousine have to do with the picture?

'They must of left out some,' she whispered to her father. 'I guess they'll have me doing some more in a minute. But they shouldn't have showed so soon how I got wounded.'

Even now she did not realize the truth – that she was in the prologue and the prologue was over. She saw Miss Blue Ribbon standing in front of her father's store and then she saw her shopping in the Blue Ribbon aisles. Now she was in a limousine again bound for the fashionable avenue, and later in a beautiful evening dress she was dancing with many young men in the ballroom of the big hotel.

In the dim light Gracie looked at her program. 'Miss Virginia Blue Ribbon,' it stated, 'representing the Queen of Today.'

'They must be saving some of that western stuff for the end,' Gracie said in an uncertain voice.

Solution

Both texts use mostly main clauses when they describe events on the screen. The part of the text which describes the experience of watching the film is reproduced below, divided into clauses. For Text 9, the representation of the music has been placed alongside: (MCl = main clause, SCl = subordinate clause, NP = noun phrase – see below).

(*) This is a noun phrase functioning as if it was a main clause.

TEXT 9

MCl 1	They were in cinema	
MCl 2	Band played tune	
		tum tum did dee dee
MCl 3	She hugged Dale's arm	
MCl 4	She jumped her knees to the time	
MCl 5	Couple on screen danced in ball-room there	
MCl 6	She did not see them	
		Dee dee did da
		Tum tum tum tum tum
MCl 7	Dale did not budge	
		Dee dee de did dee
MCl 8	She hummed now	
MCl 9	She rolled his arm between her palms	
		Da da did dee
		did dee dee tum, ta
(...)		
		Did dee dee tum ta
MCl 10	Tune was over	
MCl 11	She clapped hands	
MCl 12	and clapped	
MCl 13	Applause was general	
MCl 14	But film did not stop there oh no	
MCl 15	heroine's knickers slipped down slinky legs in full floor	
(...)		
MCl 16	And band took encore then	
		Tum tum ti tumpy tum
MCl 17	Lily arranged her hair	
		Dum dum di dumpy dum
MCl 18	She hummed then	
MCl 19	She moved her knees in time	
MCl 20	Heroine's father struggled with policeman now in full ballroom	
MCl 21	She did not watch	
MCl 22	but jumped her knees now	

                                                   Da da did DEE
                                                   (what a pause!)
                                                   did dee dee tum ta

NP 23   Great clapping of hands (*)
MCl 24   Attendant moved up gangway
MCl 25   and shouted 'Order please'
MCl 26   He moved down
(...)
MCl 27   She hummed tune
SCl 28   band was now playing

                                                   whey widdle o

(...)
MCl 29   She looked at screen
MCl 30   She saw
SCl 31   heroine's knickers again were
          coming down, now in young
          man's bedroom
(...)
MCl 32   The band played that tune

                                                   Tum tum ti tumpy tum
                                                   Dum dum di dumpy dum

MCl 33   She jumped her knees to time

                                                   Da da DID DEE

MCl 34   (it wasn't her knickers after all)

                                                   did dee dee tum ta

TEXT 10
(...)
MCl 1   There were the Indians in the distance now
(...)
MCl 2   The battle
SCl   3   looking desperately real
MCl 2   was in full swing
(...)
MCl 4   And here was the climax already
MCl 5   A savage rode up threateningly
          Bang!
MCl 6   And Gracie or someone ... [*continued*]
SCl   7   who looked like Gracie

MCl 6   ... sank wounded to the ground

(...)

MCl 8   The Indians were driven off

MCl 9   a hearty prayer was said by all

MCl 10   and the fields were expeditiously plowed for corn

MCl 11   Then, to Gracie's astonishment, the whole scene began to change

MCl 12   The suburban plain disappeared

MCl 13   and one of the covered wagons faded before her eyes into a handsome limousine

MCl 14   From the limousine stepped out a modern young girl in a fur coat with hat to match

MCl 15   It was none other than Miss Virginia Blue Ribbon the pretty daughter of the owner of the Blue Ribbon store

(...)

MCl 16   She saw Miss Blue Ribbon

SCl 17   standing in front of her father's store

MCl 18   and then she saw

SCl 19   her shopping in the Blue Ribbon aisles

MCl 20   Now she was in a limousine again bound for the fashionable avenue

MCl 21   and later in a beautiful evening dress she was dancing with many young men in the ballroom of the big hotel

(...)

ATTRIBUTION

Text 9   Henry Green, *Living*, pp. 22–3.

Text 10   Zelda Fitzgerald, 'Our Own Movie Queen', from *The Collected Writings*, pp. 284–5.

Verdict

Both texts describe the effect of a person watching a moving picture in the days before sound. Both use a series of main clauses to do this. Green doesn't attempt to link his clauses, but leaves most of them unjoined. Fitzgerald coordinates several of her clauses with *and*, and uses adjectives and prepositional phrases to mitigate the starkness of so many contiguous main clauses. In both cases, the string of main clauses presents rapidly changing action, which mimics the flickering speed of early silent films.

Green's text reads uneasily for other reasons. He omits articles where we would usually expect them, for example, 'They were in (the) cinema. (The) Band played (a) tune'; and he includes some unusual prepositional phrases, for example, 'in full floor', 'in full ballroom'. The omission of the definite article is not confined to this extract but occurs throughout the novel, whereas the phrase 'in full . . .' happens when describing a particular shot – that is, a long shot, as opposed to a close-up.

Contemporary viewers obviously had to work quite hard to keep up with the plot of silent films. Lily Gates doesn't really bother, and only watches the screen in between swaying along to the music and talking to Jim. Gracie tries to follow, but keeps having her expectations confounded as the plot develops too rapidly. Both authors convey the viewers' trouble in maintaining orientation by a high frequency of **deictic** terms. 'Deictic' means 'pointing'; that is, words which shift their referent according to context. For example, the word *here* does not refer to any fixed place, but shifts its referent according to where the speaker is placed when uttering it. It's a 'pointing' word in that *here* points to a particular place every time it is used. Texts 9 and 10 contain (amongst others) the following deictic terms:

> *Text 9*   there (2), now (5), then (2), again (2)
> *Text 10*   there (2), now (3), then (2), again (2), later (1), here (1)

So much jumping about in time and place happens on the screen that the viewers are continually surprised by it. Green reinforces this truncated effect by means of simple verb phrases (see 2.3), containing a simple past tense. Just like clauses, it is normal for authors to use the full range of compound tenses and heavy verb phrases, so for Green to use only unco-ordinated main clauses containing only simple past-tense verb phrases is very marked indeed. To some readers, it may prove so alienating as to be almost unreadable; to others, it will be exhilaratingly adventurous.

SUMMARY

Both texts convey the experience of sitting in a cinema in the 1920s watching a silent film, by juxtaposing a string of short main clauses. There is no time for subordination or elaborate modification, and a heavy use of deixis is needed to maintain orientation. The experience is shown to be noisy, hectic and demanding.

3.10   Coordination

Definition

Coordination is a process of linkage which does not differentiate between the two elements linked, for example:

> I bought   *apples* and *oranges*.
> I bought   *oranges* and *apples*.

Coordination is often signalled by the presence of *and*, but this is not necessary:

> I bought   *bananas, apples, oranges*.
> I bought   *apples, oranges, bananas*.

Where a linking word is present, the coordination is **syndetic**; when it is absent, it is **asyndetic**.

Coordination can link either noun phrases,

> aswirl with   (*porters*) and (*guides*) and (*officials*)

or whole clauses:

> (*I came in over the pole*)   and   (*we were stacked up for nearly twenty minutes in a holding circuit over London*)

133

When it links clauses, coordination contrasts with subordination, where there is some implication that the clauses that are linked are not of equal importance:

> we were stacked up for nearly twenty minutes in a holding circuit round London (*before they could find us a runway*)

Here the second clause, introduced by *before*, could not stand on its own and is subordinate.

In most texts, clauses are linked by both coordination and subordination, but the relative ratios can change dramatically depending on the style of the text.

TASK

The following text is from a travel book. In each paragraph there is a list of noun phrases. Read the whole text, then analyse the coordination of each list – why has the author used different types of coordination?

TEXT 11

Here was to be learned the importance of the guide, the man who knew local customs, the fixer to whom badly printed illiterate forms held no mysteries. 'Write here,' my guide said in the customs house, aswirl with porters and guides and officials and idlers and policemen and travellers and a Greek refugee whispering in my ear, 'Let me warn you. They are stealing tonight.' 'Write here. One Kodak.' He, the guide, indicated the dotted line marked date. 'And here,' pointing to signature, 'write no gold, ornaments or precious stones.' I objected. He said, 'Write.' He pronounced it like an Arabic word. He was tall, grave, Hollywood-sinister; he wore a fez and lightly tapped his thigh with a cane. I wrote. And it worked. 'And now,' he said, exchanging the fez marked Travel Agent for one marked Hotel X, 'let us go to the hotel.'

Thereafter, feature by feature, the East, known only from books, had continued to reveal itself; and each recognition was a discovery, as much as it had been a revelation to see the jibbah, a garment made almost mythical by countless photographs and descriptions, on the backs of real people. In the faded hotel, full, one felt, of memories of the Raj, there was a foreshadowing of the caste system. The old French waiter only served; he had his runners, sad-eyed silent Negroes in fezzes and cummerbunds, who fetched and cleared away. In the lobby there were innumerable Negro pages, pictur-esquely attired. And in the streets there was the East one had expected: the children, the dirt, the disease, the undernourishment, the cries of bakshish, the hawkers, the touts, the glimpses of minarets. There were the reminders of imperialisms that had withdrawn in the dark, glass-cased European-style shops, wilting for lack of patronage; in the sad whispering of the French hairdresser that French perfumes could no longer be obtained and that one had to make do with heavy Egyptian scents; in the disparaging references of the Lebanese business-man to 'natives', all of whom he distrusted except for his assistant who, quietly to me, spoke of the day when all the Lebanese and Europeans would be driven out of the country.

Feature by feature, the East one had read about. On the train to Cairo the man across the aisle hawked twice, with an expert tongue rolled the phlegm into a ball, plucked the ball out of his mouth with thumb and forefinger, considered it, and then rubbed it away between his palms. He was wearing a three-piece suit, and his transistor played loudly. Cairo revealed the meaning of the bazaar: narrow streets encrusted with filth, stinking even on this winter's day; tiny shops full of shoddy goods; crowds; the din, already barely supportable, made worse by the steady blaring of motor-car horns; medieval buildings partly collapsed, others rising on old rubble, with here and there sections of tiles, turquoise and royal blue, hinting at a past of order and beauty, crystal fountains and amorous adventures, as perhaps in the no less disordered past they always had done.

Solution

The first list is heavily syndetic:

> the customs house, aswirl with *porters* and *guides* and *officials* and *idlers* and *policemen* and *travellers* and *a Greek refugee whispering in my ear, 'Let me warn you. They are stealing tonight.'*

The next two more conventionally asyndetic:

> And in the streets there was the East one had expected: *the children, the dirt, the disease, the undernourishment, the cries of bakshish, the hawkers, the touts, the glimpses of minarets.*

> Cairo revealed the meaning of the bazaar: *narrow streets encrusted with filth, stinking even on this winter's day; tiny shops full of shoddy goods; crowds; the din, already barely supportable, made worse by the steady blaring of motor-car horns; medieval buildings partly collapsed, others rising on old rubble*

ATTRIBUTION

V. S. Naipaul, *An Area of Darkness*, pp. 13–14.

Verdict

As is shown in Section 1.4, lists of noun phrases are a frequent stylistic device – especially, as here, where a writer wants to describe a scene economically and slightly impressionistically. In these three lists, Naipaul uses syndetic coordination for the first, rather more heavily than is usual (given that normally we would have only one *and* in such a list), and asyndetic for the next two in a more conventional way.

The effect of the syndetic coordination in the first list is striking: each new image seems to impose itself on Naipaul's consciousness. As he says, the customs house is 'aswirl', and he is disoriented, unable to make sense of what he sees, just able to record it as a series of unrelated images.

In the two lists that follow, asyndetic coordination, and definite articles, combine with his explicit statements (it is clear that this is the East books have told him to expect) to present the images as unsurprising, almost familiar. Here, Naipaul is much more the sophisticated traveller, in control of his impressions enough to present them in a more artfully ordered narrative. He is not part of these scenes, not a confused recounter of impressions, but a distanced observer.

TASK

The following text is the opening of an espionage thriller by Adam Hall, *Tango Briefing*.

Analyse the patterns of clause linkage (*and* for coordination; *before*, *because*, *then* for subordination).

Which is the most frequent pattern?

Is this usual in texts?

What effect does it have?

TEXT 12

I came in over the Pole and we were stacked up for nearly twenty minutes in a holding circuit round London before they could find us a runway and then we had to wait for a bottle-neck on the ground to get itself sorted out and all we could do was stare through the windows at the downpour and that didn't help.

Sayonara, yes, very comfortable thank you.

There was a long queue in No. 3 Passenger Building and I was starting to sweat because the wire had said *fully urgent* and London never uses that phrase just for a laugh; then a quietly high-powered type in sharp blue civvies came up and asked who I was and I told him and he whipped me straight past Immigration and Customs without touching the sides and told me there was a police car waiting and was it nice weather in Tokyo.

'Better than here.'

'Where do we send the luggage?'

'This is all I've got.'

He took me through a fire exit and there was the rain slamming down again and the porters were trudging about in oilskins.

The radio operator had the rear door open for me and I ducked in and the driver hooked his head round to see who I was, not that he'd know.

'You want us to go as fast as we can?'

'That's what it's all about.'

Sometimes along the open stretches where the deluge was flooding the hollows we worked up quite a bow-wave and I could see the flash of our emergency light reflected in it.

'Bit of a summer storm.'

'You can keep it.'

They were using their sirens before we'd got halfway along Waterloo Road and after that they just kept their thumb on it because the restaurants and cinemas were turning out and every taxi was rolling.

Big Ben was sounding eleven when we did a nicely controlled slide into Whitehall across the front of a bus and he put the two nearside wheels up on the pavement so that I could get out without blocking the traffic.

'Best I could do.'

'You did alright.'

ATTRIBUTION

Adam Hall, *The Tango Briefing*, pp. 7–8.

Verdict

The vast majority of clauses in this text are linked by *and* (syndetic coordination) – far more than is normally the case, and this produces some very long sentences (e.g. the first paragraph). Less commonly, clauses are subordinated, normally by time (*before*, *then*) or reason (*because*) – these are the simplest methods of subordination.

The effect of this is of an uninterrupted stream of events – all sequential, all equally important, each flowing into the other in a linear narrative ordered by the rapid passage of time. The hero has been summoned from Tokyo for an urgent mission, and the syntax mirrors the urgency he feels, and creates a frantic sense of events rushing to a climax – an effective opening for a thriller.

The contribution of the syntax to the effects created by this passage could be gauged by rewriting the two heavily syndetic paragraphs beginning 'I came in . . .' and 'There was a long queue . . .' This could be done by removing the syndetic coordination:

> I came in over the Pole. We were stacked up for nearly twenty minutes in a holding circuit round London before they could find us a runway. Then we had to wait for a bottle-neck on the ground to get itself sorted out. All we could do was stare through the windows at the downpour. That didn't help.

Rewriting like this maintains the terse tone of the original, but loses the frantic sense of events piling up on one another: events seem more separate now, and time moves more slowly in the passage.

Alternatively, the coordination can be replaced with subordination:

> There was a long queue in No. 3 Passenger Building where I was starting to sweat because the wire had said *fully urgent* and London never uses that phrase just for a laugh; then a quietly high-powered type in sharp blue civvies came up asking who I was. When I told him, he whipped me straight past Immigration and Customs without touching the sides. After telling me there was a police car waiting he asked if it was nice weather in Tokyo.

This produces a much less distinctive syntax, since we are now close to the mixture of syndetic and asyndetic coordination, and subordination, which is the norm for written English.

3.11 Subordination and the sentence

Definition

So far, we have talked about clauses and clause structure, rather than sentences. This is because sentences are an artificial construct; something that we learn to build when we learn how to write.

A sentence is a string of words that begins with a capital letter, and ends with a full stop – something defined by punctuation rather than grammar.

Speakers do not speak in sentences, nor do writers write in sentences all the time. The common-sense definition of a sentence as a single idea is wide open to experimentation. Subordination allows sentences to be expanded almost indefinitely with extra clauses and ideas.

TASK

> Identify and separate the sentences and clauses in the following.
> What correlation do you find between these things?
> Why is Text 13 written in this way?

TEXT 13

Then, with Miss Worsham and the old negroes in Steven's car with the driver he had hired and himself and the editor in the editor's, they followed the hearse as it swung into the long hill up from the station, going fast in a whining lower gear until it reached the crest, going pretty fast still but with an unctuous, an almost bishoplike purr until it slowed into the square, crossing it, circling the Confederate monument and the courthouse while the merchants and clerks and barbers and professional men who had given Stevens the dollars and half-dollars and quarters and the ones who had not, watched quietly from doors and upstairs windows, swinging then into the street which at the edge of town would become the country road leading to the destination seventeen miles away, already picking up speed again and followed still by the two cars containing the four people – the high-headed erect white woman, the old negress, the designated paladin of justice and truth and right, the Heidelberg Ph.D. – in formal component complement to the negro murderer's catafalque: the slain wolf.

Solution

This text contains just one sentence: 'Then ... wolf.' It also contains just one main clause: 'they followed the hearse' – everything else is a deletable X element, mostly joined to the main clause by subordination:

SCl   (Then, with Miss Worsham and the old negroes in Steven's car with the driver he had hired and himself and the editor in the editor's,)

MCl   (they followed the hearse)

SCl   (as it swung into the long hill up from the station,)
(going fast in a whining lower gear)
(until it reached the crest,)
(going pretty fast still but with an unctuous, an almost bishoplike purr)
(until it slowed into the square,)
(crossing it,)
(circling the Confederate monument and the courthouse)
(while the merchants and clerks and barbers and professional men who had given Stevens the dollars and half-dollars and quarters and the ones who had not, watched quietly from doors and upstairs windows,)
(swinging then into the street which at the edge of town would become the country road leading to the destination seventeen miles away,)
(already picking up speed again and followed still by the two cars containing the four people – the high-headed erect white woman, the old negress, the designated paladin of justice and truth and right, the Heidelberg Ph.D. – in formal component complement to the negro murderer's catafalque: the slain wolf.)

ATTRIBUTION

William Faulkner, from *Go Down, Moses*, p. 196.

Verdict

By stretching the sentence for such a long time, Faulkner 'mimics' the slow, formal process of the funeral cortege. The 'slain wolf' is a black man who has been sentenced and executed for the crime of murder. The short story tells of his family's efforts to bring his body back home, as the only official act they can perform for him, in a society still only decades away from slavery. The grammatical sentence is a formal, official, conventional code, and by describing the stately progress of the procession within its confines, Faulkner demonstrates the black family achieving a dignity for their son in death that could not be achieved in life.

In terms of the punctuation, the whole of this passage is one sentence. Normally a sentence this long would be difficult to follow (compare the style of Henry James, Section 3.7), but here notice how the structure comes from the temporal ordering of the events – things are described in the order they happen – rather than a grammatically imposed structure of shorter sentences.

The effect of following the temporal order gives the passage its stately dignity – the writer is not using explicit argument to persuade us about the events – he apparently just displays them to us. Temporal organisation of this kind is the most basic way of ordering a text (it is common in spoken narratives) – and here its apparent simplicity adds greatly to the grace of the passage. (Imagine, for example, how Faulkner could have tried to *tell* us that the events were dignified with explicit authorial comment.)

3.12   Ambiguity in syntax

Definition

It is possible, especially in writing, to construct sentences that have more than one meaning, depending on how they are analysed and interpreted. For example,

1   Dogs must be carried on escalators.
2   All refuse here.

Does (1) mean that if you have a dog, you must carry it on the escalator, or that you must have a dog in order to go on the escalator at all? It depends not so much on syntactic structure as on the reader's knowledge of what is likely to be the intended meaning, as both meanings are structured in the same way (for propositional phrase (PP) see 3.13):

Dogs   must be carried   on escalators.
NP   VP (imperative)   PP

Does (2) mean that all rubbish is to be placed here, or that all the readers of the notice should resist here? Here meaning does depend on syntactic structure – is *refuse* a noun or a verb?

(All refuse)   here
 NP
'all rubbish is to be put here'

(All)   (refuse)   here
 NP   VP
'everybody is to resist here'

Obviously, if (2) is written over a bin, then the first meaning is the one intended, and it would be perverse to give the second interpretation. Authors can exploit both syntactic and semantic ambiguity, especially when presenting an unreliable narrator; that is, a character who conveys information to the reader that is inaccurate.

TASK

Spot the ambiguities in Text 14.
    Using Text 15 (which is the next paragraph in the same novel), can you see any other marked linguistic features that suggest why the author wrote ambiguously?

Each time I returned to Ealing, life there seemed more alien, narrow, and unattractive – and Marion less beautiful and more limited and difficult – until at last she was robbed of every particle of her magic. She gave me always a cooler welcome, I think, until she seemed entirely apathetic. I never asked myself then what heartaches she might hide or what her discontents might be. I would come home hoping nothing, expecting nothing. This was my faded life and I had chosen it. I became more sensitive to the defects I had once disregarded altogether; I began to associate her sallow complexion with her temperamental insufficiency, and the heavier lines of her mouth and nostril with her moods of discontent. We drifted apart; wider and wider the gap opened. I tired of baby-talk and stereotyped little fondlings; I tired of the latest intelligence from those wonderful workrooms, and showed it all too plainly; we hardly spoke when we were alone together. The mere unreciprocated physical residue of my passion remained – an exasperation between us.

I won't pretend to extenuate the quality of my conduct. I was a young and fairly vigorous man; all my appetite for love had been roused and whetted and none of it had been satisfied by my love affair and my marriage. I had pursued an elusive gleam of beauty to the disregard of all else, and it had failed me. It had faded when I had hoped it would grow brighter. I despaired of life and was embittered. And things happened as I am telling. I don't draw any moral at all in the matter, and as for social remedies, I leave them to the social reformer. I've got to a time of life when the only theories that interest me are generalisations about realities. To go to our inner office in Raggett Street I had to walk through a room in which the typists worked. They were the correspondence typists; our books and invoicing had long since overflowed into the premises we had had the luck to secure on either side of us. I was, I must confess, always in a faintly cloudily-emotional way aware of that collection of for the most part round-shouldered femininity, but presently one of the girls detached herself from the others and got a real hold upon my attention. I appreciated her at first as a straight little back, a neater back than any of the others; as a softly rounded neck with a smiling necklace of sham pearls; as chestnut hair very neatly done – and as a side-long glance. Presently as a quickly turned face that looked for me.

Solution

The last sentence of Text 14 is open to more than one interpretation, for example:

1 S(the residue of my passion) V(remained) X(an exasperation between us)
2 S(the residue of my passion) V(remained) *ellipted: (S(which) V(was))* X(an exasperation between us)

ATTRIBUTION

Text 14 and Text 15 H. G. Wells, *Tono-Bungay*, p. 155 (Text 14) and p. 156 (Text 15).

Verdict

The last sentence of Text 14 is syntactically ambiguous. The head of the noun phrase is *residue*, and everything preceding modifies it. *Residue* is the subject, *remained* is the verb, but what is *exasperation*? Is it a complement to *remained*, or is it a subordinate clause with *which was* understood? The dash obscures what a comma, or lack of a comma, would make clear. It could be 'my passion remained an exasperation between us', where *remain* is a transitive verb, or it could be 'my passion remained, (which was) an exasperation between us', where *remain* is intransitive, and some relative pronoun such as *which* has been omitted.

A comma would make this clear:

1   the residue of my passion remained an exasperation between us
2   the residue of my passion remained, an exasperation between us

But in Wells's text, a dash hides it; we can't tell which meaning is intended.

What are the implications of the two meanings? It highlights the two different senses of the verb *remain*. In (1) it has the sense 'to continue to be'. So to paraphrase: '. . . my passion continued to be an exasperation between us'. In other words, the narrator would be admitting that he had known all along that Marion had never desired him, but had always been exasperated by his advances. Under (2) however, the interpretation could be entirely different. This could be paraphrased as: '. . . the physical residue of my passion was left, which was an exasperation between us'. In (2), it could be the fact that it was the *residue* of the passion that is causing the exasperation, rather than the full flood of ardour. The implication here would be that Marion had desired the narrator once, that his judgement and actions had at some point been correct, but for some reason, matters had deteriorated. In other words, no comma would tell against the narrator, and he would have to accept responsibility for his error in forcing Marion into marriage; whilst a comma would exonerate him. The dash is non-committal – the narrator is not lying directly, but he's not telling the truth either.

In fact, many sentences are ambiguous, but context indicates which meaning is most likely in a given instance. As a result, we are often 'deaf' to the multiple interpretations possible. Consider the modifier *mere* in the sentence you've just been looking at in Text 14. It too has more than one interpretation:

(a)   nothing more, only, just
(b)   nothing better, simply

Meaning (a) would support interpretation (2) above, whereas meaning (b) might lead the reader to interpretation (1).

In Text 15, the narrator explains how he came to have an affair with a typist. Despite claiming 'I won't pretend to extenuate the quality of my conduct' he goes on to do just that. In the third sentence, the narrator tells how he had pursued an elusive gleam of beauty, but it failed him. So according to the narrator, it wasn't his fault. He didn't fail; the gleam of beauty did, as *gleam* is the object of the verb *pursue* and subject of the verb *fail*. In fact, 'gleam of beauty' is presumably a euphemism for Marion, so this is a way of saying 'my wife failed me, and therefore I was justified in having an affair with my typist'.

He then tells how he first became involved with the typist: 'presently one of the girls detached herself from the others and got a real hold upon my attention'. The typist didn't physically detach herself from the other typists by, for instance, getting up and moving her chair; she just became more noticeable to him. How could the typist detach herself, metaphorically? The only person who can do the noticing is the narrator. This is giving the typist an agency she can't possess; by making her the subject of the verb and by using the reflexive pronoun, 'she detached herself'. Then, she 'got a real hold' on his attention. Only the owner of the attention can know whether somebody has succeeded in getting a hold on it, but again, it is the typist who is the subject of the verb. It is presented as she who is doing the getting. She manages to do all this, just by sitting and typing a letter! This is hardly a straightforward way of putting things.

Why might Wells incorporate so many ambiguities and unclear constructions into this text? Perhaps there is an element of self-justification here, as *Tono-Bungay* is the most autobiographical of Wells's novels. Whilst a B.Sc. student at what is now Imperial College, University of London, Wells married his cousin. Within four years they were divorced.

3.13 Prepositions

Definition

Prepositions are short words. They frequently answer the question 'where?'

TEST-FRAME

She walked _____ the trees

For example:

She walked
- under the trees.
- by the trees.
- near the trees.
- through the trees.
- in the trees.

This test-frame will not work for all prepositions, but it will for many.

EXAMPLES

1 the silhouette *of* a moving cat
2 Something *in* his leisurely movements
3 it was deep summer *on* roadhouse roofs
4 the secure position *of* his feet

Exercises

Identify the prepositions in the following:

1 the full bellows of the earth

2 The wind had blown off

3 the silver pepper of the stars

4 I ran the car under its shed

Comment

Prepositions (P) can link phrases together, as in

She walked under the trees
NP VP P NP

or they can form part of the verb phrase, as in

She got up

When a preposition acts as a link between two phrases, the second phrase is known as a prepositional phrase (PP), so we can analyse the first example as

(She) (walked) (under the trees)

consisting of a noun phrase (*She*), a verb phrase (*walked*) and a prepositional phrase (*under the trees*). Note that there is a further noun phrase (*the
trees*) *inside* the prepositional phrase.

Prepositional phrases usually function as adverbials and hence are
grammatically extraneous; that is, they could be moved around the
sentence, or deleted altogether. For example, *Already it was deep summer*
forms a complete sentence on its own, without the prepositional phrases.
Or, *Already on roadhouse roofs it was deep summer*, with the prepositional
phrase repositioned. Or, *In front of wayside garages and on roadhouse
roofs already it was deep summer*.

That they are grammatically extraneous does not mean that they are
semantically extraneous. On the contrary, much of the scene-setting and
atmosphere of a text can be conveyed by prepositional phrases.

TASK

Identify the prepositions in Texts 16 and 17, and consider their
purpose.

TEXT 16

Already it was deep summer on roadhouse roofs and in front of wayside
garages, where new red petrol-pumps sat out in pools of light and when I
reached my estate at West Egg I ran the car under its shed and sat for a while
on an abandoned grass roller in the yard. The wind had blown off, leaving
a loud, bright night, with wings beating in the trees and a persistent organ
sound as the full bellows of the earth blew the frogs full of life. The silhouette
of a moving cat wavered across the moonlight, and, turning my head to
watch it, I saw that I was not alone – fifty feet away a figure had emerged
from the shadow of my neighbour's mansion and was standing with his
hands in his pockets regarding the silver pepper of the stars. Something in his
leisurely movements and the secure position of his feet upon the lawn

suggested that it was Mr Gatsby himself, come out to determine what share was his of our local heavens.

TEXT 17

The sea, flattened down in the heavier gusts, would uprise and overwhelm both ends of the Nan-Shan in snowy rushes of foam, expanding wide, beyond both rails, into the night. And on this dazzling sheet, spread under the blackness of the clouds and emitting a bluish glow, Captain MacWhirr could catch a desolate glimpse of a few tiny specks black as ebony, the tops of the hatches, the battened companions, the heads of the covered winches, the foot of a mast. This was all he could see of his ship. Her middle structure, covered by the bridge which bore him, his mate, the closed wheelhouse where a man was steering shut up with the fear of being swept overboard together with the whole thing in one great crash – her middle structure was like a half-tide rock awash upon a coast. It was like an outlying rock with the water boiling up, streaming over, pouring off, beating round – like a rock in the surf to which shipwrecked people cling before they let go – only it rose, it sank, it rolled continuously, without respite and rest, like a rock that should have miraculously struck adrift from a coast and gone wallowing upon the sea. The Nan-Shan was being looted by the storm with a senseless, destructive fury: trysails torn out of the extra gaskets, double-lashed awnings blown away, bridge swept clean, weather-cloths burst, rails twisted, light-screens smashed – and two of the boats had gone already. They had gone unheard and unseen, melting, as it were, in the shock and smother of the wave. It was only later, when upon the white flash of another high sea hurling itself amidships, Jukes had a vision of two pairs of davits leaping black and empty out of the solid blackness, with one overhauled fall flying and an iron-bound block capering in the air, that he became aware of what had happened within about three yards of his back.

Solution

TEXT 16

Already it was deep summer *on* roadhouse roofs and *in front of* wayside garages, where new red petrol-pumps sat *out in* pools *of* light and when I reached my estate *at* West Egg I ran the car *under* its shed and sat *for* a while *on* an abandoned grass roller *in* the yard. The wind had blown *off*, leaving a loud, bright night, *with* wings beating *in* the trees and a persistent organ sound as the full bellows *of* the earth blew the frogs full *of* life. The silhouette *of* a moving cat wavered *across* the moonlight, and, turning my head *to* watch it, I saw that I was not alone – fifty feet *away* a figure had emerged *from* the shadow *of* my neighbour's mansion and was standing *with* his hands *in* his pockets regarding the silver pepper *of* the stars. Something *in* his leisurely movements and the secure position *of* his feet *upon* the lawn suggested that it was Mr Gatsby himself, come *out to* determine what share was his *of* our local heavens.

TEXT 17

The sea, flattened *down in* the heavier gusts, would *up*rise and *over*whelm both ends *of* the Nan-Shan *in* snowy rushes *of* foam, expanding wide, *beyond* both rails, *into* the night. And *on* this dazzling sheet, spread *under* the blackness *of* the clouds and emitting a bluish glow, Captain MacWhirr could catch a desolate glimpse *of* a few tiny specks black as ebony, the tops *of* the hatches, the battened companions, the heads *of* the covered winches, the foot *of* a mast. This was all he could see *of* his ship. Her middle structure, covered *by* the bridge which bore him, his mate, the closed wheelhouse where a man was steering shut *up with* the fear *of* being swept *over*board *together with* the whole thing *in* one great crash – her middle structure was like a half-tide rock awash *upon* a coast. It was like an *out*lying rock *with* the water boiling *up*, streaming *over*, pouring *off*, beating *round* – like a rock *in* the surf *to* which shipwrecked people cling *before* they let go – only it rose, it sank, it rolled continuously, *without* respite and rest, like a rock that should have miraculously struck adrift *from* a coast and gone wallowing *upon* the sea. The Nan-Shan was being looted *by* the storm *with* a senseless, destructive fury: trysails torn *out of* the extra gaskets, double-lashed awnings blown *away*, bridge swept clean, weather-cloths burst, rails twisted, light-screens smashed – and two *of* the boats had gone already. They had gone unheard and unseen, melting, as it were, *in* the shock and smother *of* the wave. It was only later, when *upon* the white flash *of* another high sea hurling itself *amid*ships, Jukes had a vision *of* two pairs *of* davits leaping black and empty *out of* the solid blackness, *with* one *over*hauled fall flying and an iron-bound block capering *in* the air, that he became aware *of* what had happened *within about* three yards *of* his back.

ATTRIBUTION

Text 16   F. Scott Fitzgerald, *The Great Gatsby*, p. 27.
Text 17   Joseph Conrad, *Typhoon*, pp. 43–4.

Verdict

The prepositional phrases in the first sentence of Text 16 act as a delaying tactic. Consider the effect if they are omitted:

> Already it was deep summer [ ], where new red petrol-pumps sat [ ] and when I reached my estate [ ] I ran the car [ ] and sat [ ].

> omitted: on roadhouse roofs
> in front of wayside garages
> out in pools of light
> at West Egg
> under its shed
> for a while
> on an abandoned grass roller
> in the yard

If the prepositional phrases are omitted, the text still functions grammatically and the action is conveyed, but there is no orientation. The reader doesn't know whereabouts the action happens, and as a result, cannot infer why it happens. The atmosphere is mostly lost. The passage consists of four sentences, each containing several prepositional phrases. They have the cumulative effect of delaying the new information given in the last sentence: the introduction of Gatsby. This is an effective technique for arousing interest and expectations.

One function of prepositions is to anchor a text in time or space. The plurality of the nouns in the first sentence – 'roofs', 'garages', 'petrol-pumps' – gives a generic description: it was deep summer in all these places. However, the adjectives serve to restrict the nouns – it isn't all roofs, only roadhouse roofs. It is summer not in front of all garages, but wayside garages which have new red petrol-pumps outside. What sounds like a broad statement about the season turns out to be a highly specific description of a particular location. In fact, later on in the novel, a car accident is to occur at just such a wayside garage, and a woman killed. The author is presaging events to come, and it is largely the precision of location (as conveyed by the adjectives in the prepositional phrases) which gives this text its slightly disturbing tension.

In Text 17, as well as the two kinds of prepositional function mentioned in the Comment section (reminder: introducing prepositional phrases, for example, *in the shock and smother*, *upon the white flash*; and prepositions forming part of the verb phrase, for example, *blown away*, *spread under*, *shut up*) there is a third kind in this text: prepositions as part of a compound word. Examples are *overboard*, *outlying*, *uprise*, where a preposition functions as a prefix. All three have the same function as noted in the Comment section, that is, they serve to relate the atmosphere and the surroundings to the Nan-Shan. To see this, try reading the following version of Text 17, where all the prepositions and prepositional phrases have been deleted:

> The sea, flattened [ ], would [ ]rise and [ ]whelm both ends [ ], expanding wide [ ]. And [ ] spread [ ] and emitting a bluish glow, Captain MacWhirr could catch a desolate glimpse [ ] black as ebony, the tops [ ], the battened companions, the heads [ ], the foot [ ]. This was all he could see [ ]. Her middle structure, covered [ ], his mate, the closed wheelhouse where a man was steering shut [ ] – her middle structure was like a half-tide rock [ ]wash [ ]. It was like an [ ]lying rock [ ] – like a rock [ ] – only it rose, it sank, it rolled continuously, [ ] like a rock that should have miraculously struck adrift [ ] and gone wallowing [ ]. The Nan-Shan was being looted [ ], trysails torn [ ], double-lashed awnings blown [ ], bridge swept clean, weather-cloths burst, rails twisted, light-screens smashed – and two [ ] had gone already. They had gone unheard and unseen, melting, as it were [ ]. It was only later, when [ ] Jukes had a vision [ ], that he became aware [ ].

And then compare what was contained in the prepositional phrases:

down in the heavier gusts
of the Nan-Shan
in snowy rushes
of foam
beyond both rails
into the night
on this dazzling sheet
under the blackness
of the clouds
of a few tiny specks
of the hatches
of the covered winches
of a mast
by the bridge which bore him
up with the fear of being swept overboard
together with the whole thing
in one great crash
upon a coast
with the water boiling up, streaming over, pouring off
beating round
in the surf
to which shipwrecked people cling
before they let go
without respite and rest
from a coast
upon the sea
by the storm
with a senseless, destructive fury
out of the extra gaskets
of the boats
in the shock and smother
of the wave
upon the white flash
of another high sea hurling itself amidships
of two pairs
of davits leaping black and empty
out of the solid blackness
with one overhauled fall flying and an iron-bound block
capering
in the air

of what had happened
within about three yards
of his back

It is the prepositions, and prepositional phrases, which relate the chaotic movement of the water to the ship on the sea. Compare the force of the verbs *boiling*, *streaming*, *pouring*, *beating*, which all convey rapid, continuous, forceful movement, with *boiling up*, *streaming over*, *pouring off*, *beating round*, which orientate the rapid and repeated motion as it affects the ship. They provide a kind of subjective perspective. If you omit the prepositions and prepositional phrases, you can follow the bare bones of the action, but you lose the relation of cause and effect between the typhoon and the battered ship. It becomes a factual description. With the prepositions and prepositional phrases present, all the force and movement is presented from the perspective of what it does to the ship. Text 17 is not written from the viewpoint of a first-person narrator, yet nevertheless there is a subjective immediacy about it, which stems from so many prepositions tying the typhoon on the one hand to the Nan-Shan on the other.

SUMMARY

Prepositions have an orientating function. This implies a consciousness who does the orientating, and another consciousness who is orientated (the consciousness may be a narrator or character in the text, an object, such as the Nan-Shan, or it may be that of the reader). In Text 16 the prepositional phrases described the surroundings and created suspense; in Text 17 they largely conveyed the force of the storm.

3.14   Interrogatives

Definition

An interrogative is a question which seeks a response. This can be done in several ways in English, either by using a so-called *wh-* word such as *what, who, when, why, which* or *how*; or by inverting subject and verb; or by use of a statement structure with rising intonation at the end of an utterance; or by use of a **tag**, such as *isn't it?, didn't I?, wouldn't you?*, for example:

1   Where's your ticket?
2   Have you got a ticket?
3   You have a ticket?
4   You have got a ticket, haven't you?

TEST-FRAME

Is the utterance in question seeking a response from someone?

Not everything that looks like a question is necessarily a question. *How many times have I told you to shut the door?* is a command to shut the door, not a question about number. Similarly, a statement may have interrogative force: *You look worried today* has statement structure but is probably a request for information, a little more tactfully put than the blunt *What's wrong with you today?*

EXAMPLES

1   Is it raining?
    (= interrogative, subject/verb inversion)
2   How's your brother?
    (= interrogative, *wh-* word)
3   When are you going to stop that noise?
    (= command, *Stop that noise!* An answer such as *In February* would be perverse.)

Not all utterances formed as questions necessarily seek information, and not all those that do can be answered.

Examples (1) and (2) are questions because of their structure, whereas example (3) above (*You have a ticket?*) is only a question by means of intonation (or, in written texts, the use of a question mark). In fact, by removing the tag from example (4) above (*You have got a ticket, haven't you?*), and retaining falling intonation, it is still possible to have interrogative force. However, this usage is quite strongly marked as to what kind of response is expected:

> Have you got a ticket?
> (Neutral, the answer could be yes or no.)
>
> You have got a ticket, haven't you?
> (The implication is that the speaker would be surprised were the answer to be no.)
>
> You have got a ticket.
> (If the speaker doesn't know the answer, and hence is seeking information, then this structure requires a reinforcing affirmative answer – the speaker would be extremely surprised were it to be no.)

This last type is rather difficult to comprehend out of context. The following illustration may help:

> Speaker A: Do you drive?
> Speaker B :   No, I have never been able to afford it.
> Speaker A: Do you have a car?
> Speaker B :   No, as I say, I've always been poor.
> Speaker A: But you have passed your test.
> Speaker B :   NO! As I keep trying to tell you, I haven't had the money.

Speaker *A*'s last statement has interrogative force, because the speaker is seeking information. Speaker *A* expects the last response to be 'Yes', not 'No'. This type of interrogative (that is, statement word order plus falling intonation) can only occur in a sequence of dialogue, as above. To initiate a dialogue, speakers have to select one of the other interrogative strategies, such as *wh-* forms, subject/verb inversion, or rising intonation.

Questions are a notorious area both linguistically and sociologically, as they risk transgression of customs of taboo. The above discussion and comment holds good for British English, but you may find that extra-territorial Englishes have different rules for forming interrogatives.

TASK

> Identify the questions in Texts 18 and 19.
> To whom are they addressed and what is their function?

TEXT 18

As I stand on the edge of the lake, in the evening mist, urgent words are being poured into my ears to which I must respond. Although I am still young I want to assure my interlocutor that she will not be sexually harassed in perpetuity, that when her hair becomes less abundant and her skin loses its colour and its firmness she will be able to pursue a peaceful career studying something non-sexist like physics, or better still agronomy. I do not do this because I want to remain a polite guest, and also because I do not want to fall into my old position of class enemy. 'What is that bird?' I ask, in an effort to divert this so well-meaning young woman. 'Look! The new moon!' These observations are regarded as frivolous, for there is work to be done, there are categories to be redefined, laws to be changed. And underneath it all I sense a bewilderment which I in fact share. Will we be loved, will we be saved? And if so, by what or by whom?

Self-sufficient as I am I too feel a longing which I am reluctant to ascribe to the feminine condition alone. I try to steer the conversation towards love and marriage, the substance of my talk. Is it, should it be a quest, I ask, as it is in the story? Or is that a trap, I wonder, designed to keep women passive and expectant? If they take matters into their own hands and emancipate themselves from their ancestral longings will they be disappointed? 'They will be living in the real world, assuming personhood,' declares my friend. 'I consider myself a person, not a wife or mother. Those things are important to me, but I keep them in perspective. Bob and I share everything.' But her voice is flat, as if she has made this statement many times. A critic might say that it has an obstinate sound, as if in keeping with the agenda. But I am not a critic, although it is becoming extremely difficult to convince these feminists that I am any kind of a woman.

TEXT 19

The workmen were brewing tea over a primus, stirring gobs of condensed milk into the pan which contained the boiling tea. When the Chens were twenty yards down the street the workmen began to whoop and stamp. Chen hurried his women on.

'What do the *gwai lo* sing, Brother-in-law?'
'They are singing songs, Mui.'
'What songs, Brother-in-law?'
'Their own songs, Mui.'
'Ah.'
'Don't look back, Lily.'

Lily, however, was not to be so easily denied. She turned round and with an arm through Mui's so she would not crash into a lamp post began to walk with short steps in the same direction as the others facing backwards (one of the exercises she had performed with Father in the courtyard).

    'Lily!' Chen whirled round, scandalised. But now he was also able to see that the noise the workmen were making had nothing to do with them at all but involved one of their own number who had met with an accident (Chen thought it likely from his behaviour) involving the upsetting of hot liquid, in all likelihood tea, onto a sensitive part of his anatomy. Lily tittered. Chen found nothing amusing about the man's mishap, *faan gwai* or not. In fact he felt distinct masculine solidarity with him. Did the girls realise how painful this could be? Perhaps they knew and didn't care? Knew and gloated? Chen glanced at the nape of Lily's graceful neck, one of the few parts of her body that had up till now always pleased him. He must spend more time with Man Kee, he decided, staring into that infant's open, phlegmatic eye. He couldn't approve of all this female influence.

Solution

TEXT 18

'What is that bird?'
'Look! The new moon!' (statement with interrogative force, requiring a
    response)
Will we be loved, will we be saved?
And if so, by what or by whom?
Is it, should it be a quest, as it is in the story? Or is that a trap, designed to
    keep women passive and expectant?
If they take matters into their own hands and emancipate themselves from
    their ancestral longings will they be disappointed?

TEXT 19

'What do the *gwai lo* sing, Brother-in-law?'
'What songs, Brother-in-law?'
Did the girls realise how painful this could be?
Perhaps they knew and didn't care?
Knew and gloated?

ATTRIBUTION

Text 18   Anita Brookner, *A Family Romance*, pp. 211–12.
Text 19   Timothy Mo, *Sour Sweet*, pp. 83–4.

Verdict

Anita Brookner's questions are not answered by the text, whereas Timothy Mo's character Chen answers all the questions posed. He does not necessarily answer them correctly, however. The last three questions Chen asks do not have interrogative force, because each question answers the previous one. Chen is not asking questions to verify facts; he is using the question format to form the steps in his thinking which lead him to distrust and dislike Lily. She may be innocent of the crime of gloating over distressed males. Mo uses the question format here to tell us something about the character of Chen: that he is not quick on the uptake, does not take care to check his facts, and is probably guilty of sexual prejudice.

In Text 18 the narratorial voice is that of the central character, whose name is Jane. Jane's questions, apart from the first two, are not answerable. The first two comments do not have real interrogative force, because Jane is not really interested in the responses. She is trying to change the subject of the conversation away from feminism. The subsequent questions are not answered, and we can infer that Jane is reflective, or troubled. So many unanswered, global questions give the reader the sensation of being directly addressed by a personal voice – and one has to remember that this is the voice of the fictional character Jane, rather than Anita Brookner herself.

• • •

Chapter 4

Text Structure

- 4.1 Introduction to text structure:
  cohesion and coherence   164
- 4.2 Information structure: given to new   166
- 4.3 Ellipsis   170
- 4.4 Cohesion and coherence   176
- 4.5 Coherent models: thought   179
- 4.6 Coherent models: other languages   187
- 4.7 Coherent models: speech   195

4.1 Introduction to text structure: cohesion and coherence

> Because it was raining, I picked up my coat and put it on. I went to the door and after I opened it went outside.

Cohesion is the formal, linguistic means that texts have for showing that they have structure beyond that of the clause. Cohesive devices include pronouns, repetition, ellipsis (missing things out), coordination, subordination. For example (cohesive devices in italics):

> *Because*(1) it was raining, I picked up *my*(2) coat *and*(3) put *it*(4) on. *I*(5) went to the door *and*(3) *after*(6) *I*(5) opened *it*(4) *(7)* went outside.

1   subordinating conjunction – links two clauses by cause and effect;
2   varied reference to first person (*I–my*) – links by shared referent;
3   coordinating conjunction – links two clauses;
4   pronoun replacement – links by shared reference to previously mentioned noun phrase;
5   repetition of pronoun – links by shared referent;
6   subordinating conjunction – links two clauses by time of event;
7   ellipted pronoun (*I*) – links by shared reference to previously mentioned noun phrase.

The **coherence** of the above passage lies in less formal links, such as the logical connections between rain and coat-wearing, doors and opening them. The passage also coheres in that it conforms to our notions of what a first-person narrative should be like: tense is consistent, and the series of actions presented is both logical in terms of cause and effect (rain–coat-wearing–going outside) and temporal order.

Note that passages can have cohesion without coherence:

> Because I opened the door I went to it. It was raining. I put my coat on. I picked it up. I went outside.

And coherence without formal markers of cohesion:

> Rain. I put my coat on. Outside the air tasted fresh.

Just as clauses have an internal syntax (SVX) and typical patterns of connectivity, so texts show organisational structures. These can consist of formal linguistic features (when they produce *cohesion*) or they may consist of less formal devices based on such things as field of vocabulary choice, structural mimicry of other text types, predictability of form (when they produce coherence). There is overlap between cohesion and coherence, and between text and clause structure (as covered in Chapter 3) – all of these elements contribute towards making the difference between a random collection of words and a **text**.

Although it is usually possible to distinguish between cohesive and coherent devices, this can sometimes be difficult. However, because they share the same function (that of creating texts) it is not always necessary to distinguish them – they are formally rather than functionally different, and for this reason we will consider them together here.

Reference: cohesion and coherence

Pronoun replacement, repetition, variation, and ellipsis are all cohesive devices which work by repeated reference to something within the text. This reference can be either forwards:

> *He* was sixteen years old. *He* had unwashed brown hair . . . *Benny* rode the length of the counter on a six-wheeled brown swivel chair.

or backwards:

> *Those eyes* were like gas jets in a rust-flaked pipe. *They* informed everything you felt about him.

(both from the opening page of Peter Carey's *The Tax Inspector*). The key is that we can recover the referent of the cohesive marker from within the text itself. Typically, speech tends to use more pronoun replacement and ellipsis than writing. This is because speech takes place within a context – we can check with the speaker who they mean. Writing, unless it is being deliberately obscure, has to be more explicit.

Coherence: structural mimicry/ predictability of form

Literary texts often seek coherence by more or less elaborate ways of pretending to be other texts – reproducing their typical patterns of vocabulary, syntax, or even physical form.

Thus we have the diary or epistolary novel, or the use of a series of text types, or, more complexly, the language of non-literary texts can be used – dialect or speech (see 2.1, for an example of how the spoken-language-based idiolect of the narrator in Graham Swift's *Waterland* gives coherence to the novel). Effects created at this level of text structure are harder to tie down than those covered under vocabulary, noun phrases verb phrases or syntax – but tend to be more far-reaching in terms of how fictions work as wholes. It is at this level that traditional literary criticism works under the heading of 'genre'. A novel may have the coherence typical of a conversation, a letter, a thriller, science fiction, the Bible – these can all be subsumed under the notion of 'genre'.

4.2 Information structure: given to new

Definition

Within clauses, given information (things we already know about from previous clauses, or things we can take for granted) tends to come first, with new information held over for as long as possible. This arrangement aids understanding, as it means that readers move from things they know about, to things they don't know about.

A consequence of this arrangement is that S elements tend to be given information, and X elements new. A further tendency is for given (S) elements to be small, and new (X) to be large because if something has already been mentioned it can be represented economically by a short noun phrase (for example a pronoun). With new information, however, we want as much information as possible – so noun phrases in new slots tend to be expanded with modification.

As clauses are put together to form texts, there is a natural tendency for elements which are new/X/large to reappear in the following clause as given/S/small, for example:

S	V	X		S	V	X
They	looked	at the high glass tower.		It	shone	in the sun.
given		*new*		*given*		*new*

These regular patterns of information structure function to give texts coherence and cohesion.

Of course, these tendencies in informational structure are simply that – tendencies. To avoid monotony, and produce stylistic effects, writers employ variations on these basic patterns.

TASK

Analyse the informational structure of Text 1 in terms of given and new, pronoun replacement, expansion and reduction of noun phrases.

How does this fit with the stylistic effect of the text? (For example, follow through subsequent mentions of proper names – what kind of structures do they appear in first, and what subsequently?)

TEXT 1

It was Winston Churchill who was responsible for Clive Peacock becoming a postman.

When Churchill resigned the premiership in 1955 he was succeeded by his deputy, Anthony Eden. Eden's post at the Foreign Office was filled by Harold Macmillan, who in turn vacated the Ministry of Defence. Selwyn Lloyd, the Minister of Supply, was moved across to Defence, and Reginald Maudling from the Treasury was moved to Supply. Sir Edward Boyle, the Parliamentary Secretary in Supply, took over Mr Maudling's job, and F. J. Errol MP stepped up into Boyle's.

Unable now to devote enough time to his responsibilities on the board of Ashanti Goldfields, Mr Errol resigned his directorship of that company. Ashanti Goldfields quickly found his successor in Mr Leonard Fowey, an accountant with Financial Consultants Mayhew and Barber. Mayhew and Barber advertised for a replacement in *The Times*. Robert Haines from Norfolk applied and was appointed. He announced his departure from the post of Financial Manager at Simpsons Glue Manufacturers of Norwich with unrestrained glee, telling them they could stick their job, which was an old company joke but he couldn't resist it.

The vacancy at Simpsons was duly advertised and it caught the eye of one David Eames, a senior rep from Huntley and Palmer Biscuits in Reading. Tired of a salesman's life on the road, and looking for something more office-based, David Eames applied to Simpsons, was interviewed and was told he was totally unsuitable. However, they did have another vacancy in quality control which they thought he might like. David said he would like it very much thank you, and he and his family left Reading to put down roots in Norfolk.

Huntley and Palmer promoted an area rep to the position of senior rep. A junior rep was promoted to area rep, thus leaving a vacancy for a junior rep. Huntley and Palmer gave it to the local employment exchange to fill. The job eventually went to Patrick Bolger from South Wales, a man who had secretly always wanted to work with biscuits.

Bolger's job in a car showroom on the outskirts of Swansea was filled by Eddie Rowley, an assistant delivery manager from a Royal Mail sorting office on the Dorset coast, who had moved to South Wales when his wife inherited a guesthouse there. His job at the sorting office was filled by internal promotion, by the chief facer-canceller. A postman higher-grade was promoted to the facer-canceller tables. A postman lower-grade was promoted to postman higher-grade. This left a vacancy for a postman lower-grade. The job was advertised in the local press and a woman named Gwen Peacock drew a circle around it and shoved it under the nose of her seventeen-year-old, Clive.

Clive Peacock wrote off just to please his mother. An application form came back. Under hobbies Clive wrote cycling and natural history. He made up the bit about natural history.

═══════════════════════════

Solution

noun phrase replacement/reduction:

    new: Winston Churchill
    given: Churchill, he

    new: his deputy, Anthony Eden
    given: Eden

    new: Reginald Maudling
    given: Mr Maudling

    new: Sir Edward Boyle
    given: Boyle's

    new: F. J. Errol MP
    given: Mr Errol

    new: Robert Haines from Norfolk
    given: he

    new: one David Eames, a senior rep from Huntley and Palmer Biscuits in Reading
    given: David Eames, he, David

    new: Patrick Bolger from South Wales, a man who had secretly always wanted to work with biscuits
    given: Bolger

ATTRIBUTION

Mark Wallington, *The Missing Postman*, pp. 1–2.

Verdict

This passage is concerned with a long chain of cause and effect, extending through time and many layers of society, some real, some (presumably) fictional. Note that the causes correspond to given information, and the effects to new, and that the effect of one clause becomes the cause of the next.

The passage illustrates the tendency for things to appear first as X elements, with expanded noun phrases, and then to reappear as S elements with pronoun replacement, or reduced modification – note, for example, how *Patrick Bolger from South Wales, a man who had secretly always wanted to work with buscuits* becomes just *Bolger* as it shifts from new to given.

The effectiveness of the passage arises out of its following the given–new pattern much more closely than is usual, but note that even here there is much variation in terms of reference. As was said before, the positioning of given and new information is a tendency, not a rule.

4.3   Ellipsis

Definition

Ellipsis is a cohesive device involving the absence of an item which the reader or listener has to supply. The cohesive link is set up by the process of referring back to recover the missing item (as in pronominal reference):

How was Spain?   I didn't go ____

(where *to Spain* is ellipted). Ellipsis can also be used to set up coherent links when the item to be supplied comes from the reader's general knowledge or common sense, rather than the actual text.

Ellipsis is common in speech as a device for economy, but its use in writing treads a fine line between economy and incoherence (where too little information undermines understanding).

Note the ellipses in Texts 2 and 3.
    To what extent are they a product of the type of language being represented, and to what extent do they constitute a deliberate stylistic effort by the writer?

But the situation, once again, was due to collapse into anti-climax. In answer to his unnecessarily firm and prolonged ring at the bell, the front door was opened by a plump, grave man of about thirty-five. It was Robert Tharkles, the husband of Sheila's elder sister Edith. His expression of gravity deepened into positive melancholy, tinged with irritation, at the sight of Charles. This fool again! And the fool had still not smartened himself up! When was he going to smarten himself up?

'Sheila isn't here,' he said without waiting for Charles to say anything, and without any greeting.

'Mind if I come in all the same? Come some distance,' muttered Charles.

'There's only Edith and me here,' said Robert, as if warning Charles that by coming in he was exposing himself to an unpleasant ordeal; which was true.

Without answering, Charles levered himself past Robert and went into the hall. Edith came out of the kitchen and confronted him. 'Sheila isn't here,' she said. 'Know,' said Charles, speaking too quickly to be fully intelligible. 'Robert told me. Mind if come in perhaps cup of tea? Or when Sheila be back wanted to see her if I could.'

Under their patronising and hostile stares he pulled himself together, walked into the kitchen, and sat down on a chair.

This was typical of all the interviews Charles had ever had with Robert and Edith. It was not because he was unsuccessful that they objected to him;

lack of success, in their eyes, was not a punishable offence; one simply left such people alone. What annoyed them was that he did not even seem to be trying. Though they could not have put it into words, their objection to him was that he did not wear a uniform. If he had worn the uniform of a prosperous middle-class tradesman, like Robert, they would have approved of him. If, on the other hand, he had seriously adopted the chic disorder of the Chelsea Bohemian, they would at least have understood what he was at. In their world, it was everyone's first duty to wear a uniform that announced his status, his calling and his ambitions: from the navvy's thick boots and shirtsleeves to the professor's tweeds, the conventions of clothing saw to it that everyone wore his identity card where it could be seen. But Charles seemed not to realize the sacred duty of dressing the part.

TEXT 3

'I will ask you once more. It is the last time. Will you or will you not?'

'I will not. It is also the last time. It must be the last.'

'You will not give me your reasons?'

'I will give you one. You have too much. Your house and your land. Your parents and your sister. Your sister who is also your friend. Your work and your growing name. I like things to be on a moderate scale. To have them in my hands and not be held by them.'

'That is not the only reason. There must be a deeper one.'

'There is. And it may be deep. I do not want to marry. I seldom say so, to be disbelieved.'

'You don't feel that marriage would mean a fuller life?'

'I don't want the things it would be full of. Light words are sometimes true.'

'Then there must be a change. I do want to marry. I want to have descendants. I want to hand down my name. I could not keep up our relation under a wife's eyes. It has escaped my parents.'

'Your father I daresay. What about your mother?'

'I am not sure. It is hard to know.'

'It has not escaped her, or you would know. Silence has its use.'

The speaker's indifference to convention appeared in her clothes, her cottage, and her habit of looking full at her companion and voicing her thought. She was a short, fair woman of about thirty, with a deep voice, a strongly cut face, and calm eyes that were said to see more than other people's, and sometimes did. Her companion was a large, dark man, with solid, shapely features, heavy, gentle, nervous hands, strong, sudden movements and a look of smouldering force. He ignored convention in another way, and in one that was his own. A consciousness of being a known and regarded figure showed in his dress and his bearing, and was almost undisguised. The breach of family tradition involved in his leading a writer's life in addition to a landowner's, enhanced him in his own eyes and supported his conception of himself.

'Well, this is a last occasion. It becomes one. It is what you choose.'

'And what you do. I think you will be happy. And I hope she will. That is where the question lies.'

'If I marry her, she should be. I will do my part.'

'It will be easier than hers. I wonder if you know it.'

'Hers cannot be what yours would be. I am helpless there.'

'So am I. I am not fitted for ordinary domestic life.'

'So I must live with someone who is. And I shall not see the life as ordinary. None is so to me.'

'How do you see your own life? It is even less so to you?'

'It is as it is. As I am what I am. I know I am a man of full nature. I know I am built on a large scale. I am not afraid to say it.'

'It is true that most people would be. If I thought it of myself, I should. So you can't know if I think it. But do you know anyone who thinks he is built on a small scale?'

'I know many people who are. It is part of their interest to me.'

'But not of their interest to themselves. Do they know on what scale they are?'

'I am to marry someone who is on a moderate one, and who knows it.'

'Then I guess who it is. There is someone of whom it is true. And there would not be anyone else.'

'My father perhaps?'

'But you can hardly marry him, Hereward.'

Solution

TEXT 2

'[*Do you*] Mind if I come in all the same? [*I have*] Come some distance,' muttered Charles.

'[*I*] Know,' said Charles, speaking too quickly to be fully intelligible.

'Robert told me [*she wasn't here*]. [*Do you*] Mind if [*I*] come in perhaps [*I could have a*] cup of tea? Or [*could you tell me*] when Sheila [*will*] be back [*I*] wanted to see her if I could.'

ATTRIBUTION

Text 2   John Wain, *Hurry on Down*, pp. 15–16.

Verdict

TEXT 2

The ellipsis here comes wholly within the speech of one character – where it represents his perturbance and mood. Note that almost all of this ellipsis involves the omission of auxiliary verbs and subject pronouns – which suggests that it is rule-governed in some way. Subject pronouns and auxiliaries are deleted in spoken English quite frequently, but this usage is particularly associated with upper-middle-class spoken English. In this text, it demonstrates both the hastiness of the character Charles, and also his disinclination to engage with Edith and Robert whilst he waits for Sheila.

ATTRIBUTION

Text 3   Ivy Compton-Burnett, *A God and His Gifts*, pp. 5–7.

Verdict

TEXT 3

There is so much ellipsis in this passage that it borders on the incoherent. Amazingly, this is the opening of a novel (the main ellipses are numbered):

> 'I will ask you (1) once more. It is the last time (2). Will you or will you not (3)?'
> 'I will not (4). It is also the last time (5). It must be the last (6).'

1   not recoverable from context for several lines: 'to marry me';
2   'I will ask you';
3   not recoverable for several lines: 'marry me';
4   not recoverable for several lines: 'marry you';
5   'I will tell you';
6   'time'.

Note that in this passage, as in John Wain, *Hurry on Down*, ellipsis is most frequent in speech. Here though, two characters, rather than one, are employing it, and the range of things ellipted is much wider. Even though ellipsis is more common in actual speech than in writing, it is difficult to imagine a real conversation using it this much, and in this way. Conversation is usually much more wordy!

This highly ellipted style would seem to be a deliberate choice on the part of Compton-Burnett – as will be confirmed by reading any of her other novels. The effect is to involve the reader as much as possible in creating the meaning of the text – hence the use of dialogue rather than omniscient narration, the high frequency of ellipsis, and the even higher frequency of pronoun replacement – another feature of cohesion which relies on the reader to supply the referent. Note the pronouns in this section:

> 'Well, *this* is a last occasion. *It* becomes *one. It* is what *you* choose.'
> 'And what *you* do. *I* think *you* will be happy. And *I* hope *she* will. *That* is where the question lies.'
> 'If *I* marry *her, she* should be. *I* will do *my* part.'
> '*It* will be easier than *hers. I* wonder if *you* know *it.*'
> '*Hers* cannot be what *yours* would be. *I* am helpless there.'

particularly the shifting reference of *it*. Some readers will find this style alienating, as it requires considerable effort to read; whilst other readers will relish the logical, unflappable, pedantic trait of the speakers. One of the most unusual features of Compton-Burnett's writing is that she does not attempt to differentiate between her characters in terms of their spoken styles. Usually, authors try to create characters with identifiable personalities through slight differences in their idiolects (see Wain's characters above). In Compton-Burnett's writing, however, characterisation is subordinated to a fascination with logic; and, delightfully, all the characters speak in this way, from the lord and lady of the manor to the children and the servants. When considering the writing of Raymond Chandler (see 2.3), we remarked that his distinctive stylistic trait was his terse handling of the verb phrase; Compton-Burnett's style lies in her manipulation of ellipsis.

4.4   Cohesion and coherence

Definition

Cohesion involves formal linguistic links between sections of a text – things which can be listed, pointed at, classified. Coherence is more difficult to define or analyse since it refers to the way we know a text gels together – continuity of theme, cause and effect, and so on.

Cohesion is a surface feature – we recognise it immediately. Coherence, especially if cohesive features are rare in a text, may only emerge slowly. By delaying our realisation of the coherence of a passage, writers can make that realisation all the more powerful.

> Read Texts 4 and 5.
>   What happens?
>   What are they about? What are the effects of the way the information is presented in each case?

– What d'you think you're doing down there? Veronica asked Jimmy Sr.

– Hang on a minute. — How's tha', Veronica?

– I'm cold. — Aah!

– What's wrong?

– Your fingernail! Get up here; I'm freezing.

– Okay. — I love you, Veronica.

– Jesus. Get out and brush your teeth. No; hang on. Do that again.

– Wha'? Tha'?

– Yeah.

– There. D'yeh like tha', Veronica?

– It's alright.

She grabbed his hair.

– Where did you learn it?

– Ah, let go!

– Where!?

– In a buke! Let go o' me!

TEXT 5

Now men, I have rubbed up against a few men in my time, but women? Oh well I may as well confess it now, yes I once rubbed up against one. I don't mean my mother, I did more than rub up against her. And if you don't mind we'll leave my mother out of all this. But another who might have been my mother, and even I think my grandmother, if chance had not willed otherwise. Listen to him now talking about chance. It was she made me acquainted with love. She went by the peaceful name of Ruth I think, but I can't say for certain. Perhaps the name was Edith. She had a hole between her legs, oh not the bunghole I had always imagined, but a slit, and in this I put, or rather she put, my so-called virile member, not without difficulty, and I toiled and moiled until I discharged or gave up trying or was begged by her to stop. A mug's game in my opinion and tiring on top of that, in the long run. But I lent myself to it with a good enough grace, knowing it was love, for she had told me so. She bent over the couch, because of her rheumatism, and in I went from behind. It was the only position she could bear, because of her lumbago. It seemed all right to me, for I had seen dogs, and I was astonished when she confided that you could go about it differently. I wonder what she meant exactly. Perhaps after all she put me in her rectum. A matter of complete indifference to me. I needn't tell you. But is it true love, in the rectum? That's what bothers me sometimes. Have I never known true love, after all?

ATTRIBUTION

Text 4   Roddy Doyle, *The Snapper*, p. 175.
Text 5   Samuel Beckett, 'Molloy', p. 53.

Each of these passages contains a description of a sexual act, yet the treatment of this subject-matter could hardly be more different. In Text 4, Doyle deliberately restricts himself almost wholly to dialogue, forcing the reader to reconstruct the events from partial evidence: in other words, to supply the coherence.

Virtually the only cohesive clues given are deictic – 'down there', 'up here', 'get out' – slowly the reader pieces them together with the reference to cleaning teeth, and Veronica grabbing Jimmy's hair to reconstruct a try at oral sex. Given the lack of cohesion, it is impossible in the early stages to know what is going on, but with suspicion and realisation, and rereading, the reader slowly works out what is happening. The delayed process of understanding here adds to the humour of the text by involving the reader.

Where Text 4 relies wholly on the reader supplying coherence, Text 5 is fully cohesive and coherent with a minimum of effort on the part of the reader. In fact, Text 5 may well be too cohesive and coherent for some readers – the taboos surrounding the depiction of sex are so strong, that we normally rely to some extent on reader-supplied coherence, rather than stating everything quite so baldly. Here the refusal to be coy or erotic is very much bound up with a refusal to use the coherent devices which allow authors to hint or gesture rather than state.

4.5 Coherent models: thought

Aside from linguistic items such as pronoun replacement and ellipsis, cohesion is created by the predictability of grammatical structures – SVX within the clause, coordination and subordination outside it.

Coherence arises out of what might be called 'common-sense' links between ideas. If we can be expected to know about the relationship, writers may be able to leave out or reduce explicit cohesive links.

Texts also gain coherence if we can recognise that they have a model which supplies structure and form – which dictates the way a text appears on the page, or the linguistic features which appear in it (the diary or epistolary novel, for example, or a section within a novel which mimics the form of another type of text or language).

> Texts 6 and 7 both show someone falling asleep.
>
> How is the supposed structure of thought being used to structure them?
>
> Are the elements linked by cohesion or coherence? How does grammatical structure function?

TEXT 6

[Note: this text is uncut: '. . .' as used in the original.]

She thought sleepily of her Wesleyan grandparents, gravely reading the *Wesleyan Methodist Recorder*, the shop at Babington, her father's discontent, his solitary fishing and reading, his discovery of music ... science ... classical music in the first Novello editions ... Faraday ... speaking to Faraday after lectures. Marriage ... the new house ... the red brick wall at the end of the garden where young peach trees were planted ... running up and downstairs and singing ... both of them singing in the rooms and the garden ... she sometimes with her hair down and then when visitors were expected pinned in coils under a little cap and wearing a small hoop ... the garden and lawns and shrubbery and the long kitchen-garden and the summer-house under the oaks beyond, and the pretty old gabled 'town' on the river and the woods all along the river valley and the hills shining up out of the mist. The snow man they both made in the winter – the birth of Sarah, and then Eve ... his studies and book-buying – and after five years her own disappointing birth as the third girl, and the coming of Harriett just over a year later ... her mother's illness, money troubles – their two years at the sea to retrieve . . . the disappearance of the sunlit red-walled garden always in full summer sunshine with the sound of bees in it, or dark from windows . . . the narrowing of the house-life down to the Marine Villa – with the sea creeping in – wading out through the green shallows, out and out till you were more than waist deep – shrimping and prawning hour after hour for weeks together . . . poking in the rock pools, watching the sun and the colours in the strange afternoons . . . then the sudden large house at Barnes with the 'drive' winding to the door . . .

TEXT 7

. . . a quarter after what an unearthly hour I suppose theyre just getting up in China now combing out their pigtails for the day well soon have the nuns ringing the angelus theyve nobody coming in to spoil their sleep except an odd priest or two for his night office the alarmclock next door at cockshout clattering the brains out of itself let me see if I can doze off 1 2 3 4 5 what kind of flowers are those they invented like the stars the wallpaper in Lombard street was much nicer the apron he gave me was like that something only I only wore it twice better lower this lamp and try again so as I can get up early Ill go to Lambes there beside Findlaters and get them to send us some flowers to put about the place in case he brings him home tomorrow today I mean no no Fridays an unlucky day first I want to do the place up someway the dust grows in it I think while Im asleep then we can have music and cigarettes I can accompany him first I must clean the keys of the piano with milk whatll I wear a white rose or those fairy cakes in Liptons I love the smell of a rich big shop at 7 ½d a lb or the other ones with the cherries in them and the pinky sugar 11d a couple of lbs of course a nice plant for the middle of the table Id get that cheaper in wait wheres this I saw them not long ago I love flowers Id love to have the whole place swimming in roses God of heaven theres nothing like nature the wild mountains then the sea and the waves rushing then the

beautiful country with fields of oats and wheat and all kinds of things and all
the fine cattle going about that would do your heart good to see rivers and
lakes and flowers all sorts of shapes and smells and colours springing up even
out of the ditches primroses and violets nature it is as for them saying theres
no God I wouldnt give a snap of my two fingers for all of their learning why
dont they go and create something I often asked atheists or whatever they call
themselves go and wash the cobbles off themselves first then go howling for
the priest and they dying and why why because theyre afraid of hell on
account of their bad conscience ah yes I know them well who was the first
person in the universe before there was anybody that made it all who ah they
dont know neither do I so there you are they might as well try to stop the sun
from rising tomorrow . . .

Solution

TEXT 6

Text 6 employs a very simple grammatical structure. Despite the
punctuation, the stream of images are all part of the same clause:

> S(She)   V(thought)   X Av(sleepily)   O/C(of her
> Wesleyan . . . to the door . . .)

The whole of this O/C element could be replaced with *this*:

> She thought sleepily of this.

and each element in it is a noun phrase or clause.

Cohesion in this piece is therefore very strong, as is coherence: there
is an autobiographical and temporal ordering in the way the images are
presented.

TEXT 7

Text 7 makes use of a range of cohesive devices, for example:

1	repetition:	tomorrow, today, Friday, day
2	pronouns:	the dust grows in *it*
3	deictic words:	*first* I want to do the place up … *then* we can have music; the *other* ones with the cherries in them
4	semantic field:	music, accompany, keys, piano
5	hyponyms:	Lambes, Findlaters, Liptons (these are all types of shop)

The clauses and phrases are linked either by syntactic or semantic means; that is, they show text cohesion. However, each new topic does not necessarily relate to the one before it or the one after it. Sometimes it may refer to the last topic but one, or it may introduce a completely new theme. In other words, the text does not really cohere. Here is the text again, this time divided up into topics:

1   a quarter after what an unearthly hour
     I suppose theyre just getting up in China now
     combing out their pigtails for the day
     well soon have the nuns ringing the angelus
     theyve nobody coming in to spoil their sleep
     except an odd priest or two for his night office
     the alarmclock next door at cockshout
     clattering the brains out of itself
2   let me see if I can doze off
     1 2 3 4 5
3   what kind of flowers are those
     they invented
     like the stars
     the wallpaper in Lombard street was much nicer
     the apron he gave me was like that
     something
     only I only wore it twice
4   better lower this lamp and try again so as I can get up early
5   Ill go to Lambes there beside Findlaters
     and get them to send us some flowers to put about the place
     in case he brings him home tomorrow today I mean

no no Fridays an unlucky day
first I want to do the place up someway
the dust grows in it I think while Im asleep
then we can have music and cigarettes
I can accompany him
first I must clean the keys of the piano with milk
whatll I wear
a white rose
or those fairy cakes in Liptons
I love the smell of a rich big shop
at 7 ½d a lb
or the other ones with the cherries in them
and the pinky sugar 11d a couple of lbs
of course a nice plant for the middle of the table
Id get that cheaper in
wait wheres this I saw them not long ago

6   I love flowers
Id love to have the whole place swimming in roses
God of heaven theres nothing like nature
the wild mountains
then the sea and the waves rushing
then the beautiful country with fields of oats and wheat and all kinds of
    things
and all the fine cattle going about
that would do your heart good to see
rivers and lakes and flowers
all sorts of shapes and smells and colours springing up
even out of the ditches
primroses and violets
nature it is

7   as for them saying theres no God
I wouldnt give a snap of my two fingers for all of their learning
why dont they go and create something
I often asked atheists or whatever they call themselves
go and wash the cobbles off themselves first
then go howling for the priest
and they dying
and why why
because theyre afraid of hell on account of their bad conscience
ah yes

I know them well
who was the first person in the universe before there was anybody that
    made it all
who
ah they dont know
neither do I
so there you are
they might as well try to stop the sun from rising tomorrow

Topic 1 = the time of day: early hours of the morning
Topic 2 = trying to get to sleep
Topic 3 = flowered wallpaper, patterned apron
Topic 4 = trying to get to sleep
Topic 5 = activities of the coming day
Topic 6 = nature
Topic 7 = theology

ATTRIBUTION

Text 6   Dorothy Richardson, *Pilgrimage*, pp. 32–3.
Text 7   James Joyce, *Ulysses*, pp. 702–3.

Verdict

Both of these texts feature the thoughts of someone as they fall asleep. Both are early experiments with what came to be known as 'stream of consciousness' – the representation of thought in a more or less impressionistic way. Richardson is generally regarded as the first writer to use the technique in English, and Joyce is probably its best-known proponent.

Note that both writers regard pure thought as being something different from the syntax of written English. Although remaining within the bounds of the clause, Richardson constructs a much longer set of asyndetic links than would be normal in most writing. Joyce departs from the norms of written syntax even more radically – unlike most other texts in this book, this text has been lifted from a long passage of continuous prose – there was no paragraph break separating this extract from its surroundings.

In Text 7, most of the clauses and phrases are cohesive with the next, or with one further back, but overall the text is not particularly coherent (in the linguistic sense of the word). The end of the text bears little relation to the beginning, other than the mention of 'tomorrow'. The narrator is following a process of thought-association, where each stimulus (for example, seeing the flowered wallpaper) sets off a chain of associated ideas.

There is no plot, in that there is no clear beginning, middle, or end; nor is it totally unstructured, in that the narrator's thoughts are ordered rather than completely random. Within each topic there are further digressions, for example:

			TOPIC
1			
	(a)	a quarter after what an unearthly hour	(the time)
	(b)	I suppose theyre just getting up in China now	(the time in China)
	(b)	combing out their pigtails for the day	(Chinese)
	(c)	well soon have the nuns ringing the angelus	(the time in the convent)
	(c)	theyve nobody coming in to spoil their sleep	(nuns)
	(c)	except an odd priest or two for his night office	(priests)
	(d)	the alarmclock next door at cockshout	(the alarm clock)
	(d)	clattering the brains out of itself	(the alarm clock)
5			
	(a)	Ill go to Lambes there beside Findlaters	(going shopping)
	(a)	and get them to send us some flowers to put about the place	(shopping)
	(b)	in case he brings him home tomorrow today I mean	(visitor, day)
	(b)	no no Fridays an unlucky day	(day)
	(c)	first I want to do the place up someway	(housework)
	(c)	the dust grows in it I think while Im asleep	(housework)
	(d)	then we can have music and cigarettes	(music)
	(d)	I can accompany him	(music)
	(d)	first I must clean the keys of the piano with milk	(music)
	(e)	whatll I wear	(dress for visitor)
	(a)	a white rose	(shopping: flowers)

(a)	or those fairy cakes in Liptons	*(shopping: cakes)*
(f)	I love the smell of a rich big shop	*(shop)*
(a)	at 7 ½d a lb	*(cakes)*
(a)	or the other ones with the cherries in them	*(cakes)*
(a)	and the pinky sugar 11d a couple of lbs	*(cakes)*
(a)	of course a nice plant for the middle of the table	*(shopping: plant)*
(a)	Id get that cheaper in	*(shopping: plant)*
(f)	wait wheres this I saw them not long ago	*(shop)*

Within each of the seven topic shifts the clauses are coherent, that is, they all make reference to the same theme. In Topic 1 above each clause or phrase refers to the time, and in Topic 5 above each clause or phrase makes reference to preparations to be made the following day in case a visitor comes. But over the text as a whole there is no coherence – there's no formal link between the topics of getting to sleep and a regard for nature, or preparing for a visit and theology.

4.6   Coherent models: other languages

Definition

A **calque** is a word or phrase which is translated directly into one language from another, retaining the structural properties of the first language. For example, English retains many calqued titles which show the influence of Norman French after the Conquest:

Princess royal
Governor general

where the adjective postmodifies the head noun in direct contradiction to normal English word order.

Languages may also influence each other in more major structural ways – with grammatical shifting.

TASK

Texts 8, 9 and 10 all show departures from expected English grammar and text structure under the influence of other languages.

Detail these departures, and suggest why the writers may have made use of them.

TEXT 8

Betty said in a low voice, 'Personally, I do not believe any hysterical talk of "world inundation" by any people. Slavic or Chinese or Japanese.' She regarded Robert placidly. She was in complete control of herself, not carried away; but she intended to express her feeling. A spot of colour, deep red, had appeared in each of her cheeks.

They ate for a time without conversing.

I did it again, Robert Childan informed himself. Impossible to avoid the topic. Because it's everywhere, in a book I happen to pick up or a record collection, in these bone napkin rings – loot piled up by the conquerors. Pillage from my people.

Face facts. I'm trying to pretend that these Japanese and I are alike. But observe: even when I burst out as to my gratification that they won the war, that my nation lost – there's still no common ground. What words mean to me is sharp contrast vis-à-vis them. Their brains are different. Souls likewise. Witness them drinking from English bone china cups, eating with U.S. silver, listening to Negro style of music. It's all on the surface. Advantage of wealth and power makes this available to them, but it's ersatz as the day is long.

Even the I Ching, which they've forced down our throats; it's Chinese. Borrowed from way back when. Whom are they fooling? Themselves? Pilfer customs right and left, wear, eat, talk, walk, as for instance consuming with gusto baked potato served with sour cream and chives, old-fashioned

American dish added to their haul. But nobody fooled, I can tell you; me least of all.

Only the white races endowed with creativity, he reflected. And yet I, blood member of same, must bump head to floor for these two. Think how it would have been had we won! Would have crushed them out of existence. No Japan today, and the U.S.A. gleaming great sole power in entire wide world.

ATTRIBUTION

Philip K. Dick, *The Man in the High Castle*, pp. 112–13.

Verdict

This text describes an American eating a meal with a Japanese couple – yet the thoughts of the American come out in an English which is reminiscent of the English spoken by Japanese speakers. The 'errors' of grammar here are in fact structural influences from Japanese. We have overly formal vocabulary:

> I did it again, Robert Childan *informed himself*

Omission of dummy subjects and *to be*:

> [*It is*] Impossible to avoid the topic

Omission of articles and determiners:

> What words mean to me is [*a*] sharp contrast vis-à-vis them. Their brains are different. [*Their*] Souls likewise. Witness them drinking from English bone china cups, eating with U.S. silver, listening to [*The*] Negro style of music. It's all on the surface. [*The*] Advantage of wealth and power makes this available to them, but it's ersatz as the day is long.

Omission of subjects (and an article and *to be*):

Even the I Ching, which they've forced down our throats; it's Chinese. Borrowed from way back when. Whom are they fooling? Themselves? [*They*] Pilfer customs right and left, wear, eat, talk, walk, as for instance [*them*] consuming with gusto baked potato served with sour cream and chives, [*an*] old-fashioned American dish added to their haul. But nobody [*is*] fooled, I can tell you; me least of all.

The reason for this strange scene of an American talking Japanese-influenced English to a Japanese couple is only fully clear in the context of the whole novel.

This is a science-fiction novel based on the assumption that Japan and Germany won World War II and divided America between them. The scene is set in Japanese-occupied San Francisco, and the narrator, who makes his living selling antiques from US history to the Japanese, is being entertained by two rich collectors. Caught between his admiration for their poise and civilisation, and resentment of their invasion and plunder of his culture, the narrator feels decidedly ambivalent about his hosts. This ambivalence is neatly caught in the final section where the narrator gives vent to a racist rant which draws ever more heavily on the structure of the language of one of the peoples he vilifies:

Only the white races [*are*] endowed with creativity, he reflected. And yet I, [*a*] blood member of [*the*] same, must bump [*my*] head to [*the*] floor for these two. Think how it would have been had we won! [*We*] Would have crushed them out of existence. [*There would be*] No Japan today, and the U.S.A. [*would be the*] gleaming great sole power in [*the*] entire wide world.

TEXT 9 ▬▬▬▬▬▬▬▬▬▬▬▬▬▬▬▬▬▬▬▬▬▬▬▬▬▬▬▬▬▬▬▬

'We want nothing of you,' a voice came from the crowd. 'We want nothing of you. We want only the man you keep in your house.'

'I keep no one. Why should I any of you keep who called me a witch and have kept me away from the town? Why should I any of you keep? Leave me alone. Go your ways,' the standing shadow strongly spoke without fear.

As the standing shadow spoke thus, a stronger voice came from the crowd. 'We go our ways? You cannot speak thus to us. Know that you are a witch be. You couldn't thus speak to us in the old times. Even now . . . .'

'Come and take me and hang me as in the old times they used to do. Come and take me,' went forth the challenge from the standing shadow.

'Give us our man,' shouted a voice.

'Which man you want of me?' asked Tuere with a strong inside.

'Give us Okolo.'

'Okolo? Why should I keep him? Is he not one of you?'

'Argue not with her,' said a voice. 'Let's enter the house and bring him out.'

'I say I keep no one. If you say the man you want is in my house, come in and take him,' said Tuere with a steady inside.

'You say he entered the forest?' asked a voice.

'I said not so. Accuse me not of what I said not,' she said.

'You heard not his footsteps?' asked another voice.

'I am used only to bad footsteps. So I only heard bad footsteps.'

ATTRIBUTION

Gabriel Okara, *The Voice*, p. 29.

Verdict

Okara is a Nigerian writer whose first language is Ijaw. His allegorical novel, *The Voice*, is written in an English deliberately calqued on the structures of Ijaw. The aim of this is to overcome the cultural associations of English – to remake the language into something capable of coping with African philosophy and folklore. In this section of the novel there is a series of features which can be traced to Ijaw.

1   adverbials placed in unusual clause slots:

We want *only* the man you keep in your house

the standing shadow *strongly* spoke without fear.
You couldn't *thus* speak to us in the old times.

2   some SOV clauses rather than SVO:

Why should I *any of you* keep who called me a witch
and have kept me away from the town? Why should I
any of you keep?

3   *be* reinforcement:

Know that you *are* a witch *be*.

4   no use of auxiliary *do*:

'Which man [*do*] you want of me?' asked Tuere with a strong inside.
'Give us Okolo.'
'Okolo? Why should I keep him? Is he not one of you?'
'[*Do not*] Argue not with her,' said a voice. 'Let's enter the house and
bring him out.'
'I say I keep no one. If you say the man you want is in my house, come
in and take him,' said Tuere with a steady inside.
'You say he entered the forest?' asked a voice.
'I [*did not say*] said not so. [*Do not accuse*] Accuse me not of what I [*did
not say*] said not,' she said.
'[*Did you not hear*] You heard not his footsteps?' asked another voice.

Note that the use of such devices is a delicate business: too little, and the
language becomes tokenist, or superficial; too much, and anglophone
readers may not follow the text. Even here, for example, it is difficult to
know what the *be*-reinforcement structure indicates: is it simply mirroring
Ijaw syntax, or is this an emphasis marker?

TEXT 10 ━━━━━━━━━━━━━━━━━━━━━━━━━━━━━━━━━━━━━━

'RETURN THE PARTS OF THE BODY TO THE OWNERS; OR HIRED PARTS OF THE COMPLETE GENTLEMAN'S BODY TO BE RETURNED'

As they were travelling along in this endless forest then the complete gentleman in the market that the lady was following, began to return the hired parts of his body to the owners and he was paying them the rentage money. When he reached where he hired the left foot, he pulled it out, he gave it to the owner and paid him, and they kept going; when they reached the place where he hired the right foot, he pulled it out and gave it to the owner and paid for the rentage. Now both feet had returned to the owners, so he began to crawl along the ground, by that time, that lady wanted to go back to her town or her father, but the terrible and curious creature or the complete gentleman did not allow her to return or go back to her town or her father again and the complete gentleman said thus:– 'I had told you not to follow me before we branched into this endless forest which belongs only to terrible and curious creatures, but when I became a half-bodied incomplete gentleman you wanted to go back, now that cannot be done, you have failed. Even you have never seen anything yet, just follow me.'

When they went furthermore, then they reached where he hired the belly, ribs, chest etc., then he pulled them out and gave them to the owner and paid for the rentage.

Now to this gentleman or terrible creature remained only the head and both arms with neck, by that time he could not crawl as before but only went jumping on as a bull-frog and now this lady was soon faint for this fearful creature whom she was following.

ATTRIBUTION

Amos Tutuola, *The Palm-Wine Drinkard*, pp. 19–20.

Verdict

As was the case with Okara's language, there are some grammatical features here which derive from Tutuola's native language, Yoruba. The passage does not seem to distinguish between the simple and the continuous in the past:

> the complete gentleman in the market that the lady was following, *began* to return the hired parts of his body to the owners and he *was paying* them the rentage money

nor does it use the past perfect as English English would:

> When he reached where he [*had*] hired the left foot, he pulled it out, he gave it to the owner and paid him, and they kept going; when they reached the place where he [*had*] hired the right foot, he pulled it out and gave it to the owner and paid for the rentage.

but note:

> Now both feet *had* returned to the owners, so he began to crawl along the ground

Possession is indicated with *to*:

> Now *to* this gentleman or terrible creature remained only the head and both arms with neck

However, the key feature of this text is not its use of Yoruba grammatical structures, but its use of the structural features of oral story-telling, derived from Tutuola's Yoruba background. Thus we have characters referred to with set epithets rather than pronoun replacement or variation:

> THE COMPLETE GENTLEMAN ... the complete gentleman ... the terrible and curious creature or the complete gentleman ... the complete gentleman ... a half-bodied incomplete gentleman ... this gentleman or terrible creature ... this fearful creature

and sections which repeat epithets and structures:

1   As they were travelling along in this endless forest then *the complete gentleman in the market that the lady was following,* began to return the hired parts of his body to the owners and he was paying them the rentage money.

this *lady* was soon faint for this fearful creature whom she *was following*

2   *When* he *reached where he hired the* left *foot, he pulled it out*, he *gave it to the owner and paid* him

when they *reached* the place *where he hired the* right *foot, he pulled it out* and *gave it to the owner and paid* for the rentage

3   *Now* both feet had returned to the owners, so he began to *crawl* along the ground

Now to this gentleman or terrible creature remained only the head and both arms with neck, by that time he could not *crawl* as before but only went jumping on as a bull-frog

4   by that time, that lady wanted to *go back to her town or her father*

but the terrible and curious creature or the complete gentleman did not allow her to return or *go back to her town or her father*

The cohesion that these repetitious structures give the text is vitally important – given that the subject-matter is so strange.

4.7   Coherent models: speech

Definition

It may seem self-evident to state that speech and writing are not the same thing. Speech is transient, unplanned; it cannot be recalled and revised. Writing is fixed, considered; it can be recast or struck out. But there are differences of structure as well as medium and context – sentences exist only on the page, the cohesive links within conversations linking topics may extend over many minutes, some grammatical structures favour one form of language over the other.

One of the defining characteristics of prose in the twentieth century has been a willingness to experiment with features which are more often found in speech, from dialect to complex patterns of grammatical organisation.

Any writer who wants to mimic or draw on speech forms is faced with a major problem. The loss of prosodic features such as stress, intonation and pauses means that written language can carry much less information than the spoken form. Either the reader or the writer has to work hard to make up this deficit.

Speech syntax: intercalated clauses

Comment

Usually, in written texts, certain units are regarded as indivisible. Hence in a noun phrase we would expect the slots to the left of the head to be filled by determiners, enumerators, adjectives, nouns or pronouns. For example:

(The five noisy naughty boys)

In speech, however, we find speakers inserting other things, in particular, clauses, within the noun phrase. For example:

(The five [and they were very noisy and naughty indeed] boys)

Speech contains many more intercalated clauses (that is, interspersed clauses) than occur in writing. This is because speakers do not speak in sentences, but in a sequence of clauses, with intonation marking the syntactic boundaries.

TASK

> Identify the intercalated clauses in Text 11.
> What effect do they give?

There was a long silence. Then she said,

'What would I 'ave to do, Arthur, on top of wearin' the things?'

'Keep the occurrience book.'

'God 'elp us, what's that?'

'Where they write the telephone messages down.'

'Oh no, not me, not much. Why, once at the Royal College, you know where I've worked these fifteen years, they said, "Mary, Miss Hofford, an' she was a nice girl you was glad to oblige, Miss O we called her's deaf to-day or I forget what, an' would you mind answering the telephone through the mornin'." I expect it was a cold she 'ad. Oh dear. Never again. I don't seem ever to get used to that instrument. Oh no. I couldn't.'

'Well then, there's the kitchen.'

'What, me cook for a 'undred? Oh my Gawd.'

Solution

Miss Hofford	=	subject of main clause 1
an' she was a nice girl	=	intercalated main clause 1
you was glad to oblige	=	intercalated subordinate clause to intercalated main clause 1
Miss O we called her	=	intercalated main clause 2
's deaf to-day	=	verb and complement of main clause 1
or I forget what	=	intercalated main clause 2
an' would you mind	=	main clause 3
answering the telephone through the mornin'	=	subordinated noun clause to main clause 3

The clauses can be built up in sequence:

[(they) (said), ['Mary, Miss Hofford's deaf to-day an' would you mind answering the telephone through the mornin'.']

they said, 'Mary, Miss Hofford, [an' she was a nice girl]'s deaf to-day an' would you mind answering the telephone through the mornin'.'

they said, 'Mary, Miss Hofford, [an' she was a nice girl [you was glad to oblige]]'s deaf to-day an' would you mind answering the telephone through the mornin'.'

they said, 'Mary, Miss Hofford, [an' she was a nice girl [you was glad to oblige]] [Miss O we called her]'s deaf to-day an' would you mind answering the telephone through the mornin'.'

they said, 'Mary, Miss Hofford, [an' she was a nice girl [you was glad to oblige]] [Miss O we called her]'s deaf to-day [or I forget what], an' would you mind answering the telephone through the mornin'.'

ATTRIBUTION

Henry Green, *Caught*, pp. 53–4.

Verdict

Henry Green was a highly experimental novelist, as his frequent appearances in this book suggest. Many of his experiments with English prose involve the importation of acutely observed spoken features. Here Green captures a series of intercalated clauses – something which would be easy to follow if heard, because intonation would make the syntactic boundaries clear, but which is very difficult to follow on the page.

This should prove that the grammar of speech is not 'simpler' or more basic than that of written English – in fact, it is often much more difficult to analyse.

Speech syntax: coordination and relative clauses

Comment

Although subordination is not absent from spoken English, it is more usual to find clauses linked by coordination, or simply interleaved as in the intercalated clauses examined above. Typically stretches of spoken language consist of a series of main clauses linked with *and* or *then* – very often in a temporal sequence.

The most common kind of subordination in speech is probably relativisation. Relative clauses occur in slot 4 of the noun phrase, postmodifying the noun:

```
That   is   (the   young   man   (who I know))
             1     2       3     4
That   is   (the   young   man   (that I know))
             1     2       3     4
That   is   (the   young   man   (I know))
             1     2       3     4
```

As the examples show, they can be introduced by *who* (or *which*), *that*, or nothing at all. The different ways of beginning relatives carry different levels of formality – the *wh-* relatives are the most formal, the *that* and *nothing* relatives less so. *Wh-* relatives are more common in written English, the other types more common in the spoken language.

TASK

Identify the patterns of clause linkage and the relatives in the following text.

Why does the author use these patterns?

And at this time I had a nanny that was William's sister, that had run away from home and so she had to be a nanny, but very vigorous and affectionate was this nanny, that was called Elizabeth, and very strongly indeed she took to my mama, and very strongly indeed she raged against my papa that was to her villain of the villa. She would not have one good word said for my papa but was always shaking her head and saying: If the truth were known, and: It can come to no good. And: There will be trouble. So very soon I began too to rage very furiously against my papa. I sat upright in my baby-carriage and wished mama hadn't made such a foolish marriage.

Solution

Clause linkage (not including relative clauses):

Main clause	*And* at this time I had a nanny that was William's sister, that had run away from home
Subclause	*and so* she had to be a nanny,
Main clause	*but* very vigorous and affectionate was this nanny, that was called Elizabeth,
Main clause	*and* very strongly indeed she took to my mama,
Main clause	*and* very strongly indeed she raged against my papa that was to her villain of the villa.
Main clause	She would not have one good word said for my papa
Main clause	*but* was always shaking her head and saying:
3 Subclauses	(coordinated under 'saying'):
	If the truth were known,
	and: It can come to no good.
	And: There will be trouble.
Subclause	*So* very soon I began too to rage very furiously against my papa.
Main clause	I sat upright in my baby-carriage
Main clause	*and* wished mama hadn't made such a foolish marriage.

Relatives:

(a nanny (that was William's sister), (that had run away from home))

(this nanny, (that was called Elizabeth))

(my papa (that was to her villain of the villa))

ATTRIBUTION

Stevie Smith, *Novel on Yellow Paper*, pp. 74–5.

Verdict

This text seeks to reproduce the speech of a child – the syntactic techniques it uses are relatively straightforward. Generally coordination is used rather than subordination, so the repetition of *and* becomes rather insistent. The most frequent type of subordination in the passage is relativisation, which is the most frequent type of subordination in speech, and the text also uses, again to the point of over-insistence, *that*, the less formal relativiser. All of this provides the foundation for the humour of the text: a baby judging its parents' marriage.

●   ●   ●

Chapter 5

Vocabulary

- 5.1 Introduction to vocabulary 204
- 5.2 Register: use of romance vocabulary 209
- 5.3 Register: use of 'long' words 213
- 5.4 Word-formation: bound morphemes 215
- 5.5 Romance 220
- 5.6 Semantic fields 222
- 5.7 Collocation 227
- 5.8 Synonyms 230

5.1 Introduction to vocabulary

Take almost any piece of current English, look the words up in an etymological dictionary (one which tells you which language the words come from and when they entered the language), and you will find that 'current' English is a mixture of words derived from different languages at different times.

The paragraph you have just read, for example, looks like this when you add the source language and the date of first recorded use:

Take	(Old Norse, c.1100)	*almost*	(Old English, before 1000)
any	(Old English, before 1000)	*piece*	(Old French, 1225)
of	(Old English, before 1000)	*current*	(Old French, 1300)
English	(Old English, before 1000)	*look*	(Old English, before 1000)
the	(Old English, before 1000)	*words*	(Old English, before 1000)
up	(Old English, before 1000)	*in*	(Old English, before 1000)
an	(Old English, before 1000)	*etymological*	(Latin, 1592)
dictionary	(Latin, 1526)	*one*	(Old English, before 1000)
which	(Old English, before 1000)	*tells*	(Old English, before 1000)
you	(Old English, before 1000)	*which*	(Old English, before 1000)
language	(Old French, 1290)	*the*	(Old English, before 1000)
words	(Old English, before 1000)	*come*	(Old English, before 1000)

from	(Old English, before 1000)	*and*	(Old English, before 1000)
when	(Old English, before 1000)	*they*	(Old Norse, 1200)
entered	(Old French, 1300)	*the*	(Old English, before 1000)
language	(Old French, 1290)	*and*	(Old English, before 1000)
you	(Old English, before 1000)	*will*	(Old English, before 1000)
find	(Old English, before 1000)	*that*	(Old English, before 1000)
'current'	(Old French, 1300)	*English*	(Old English, before 1000)
is	(Old English, before 1000)	*a*	(Old English, before 1000)
mixture	(Latin, 1530)	*of*	(Old English, before 1000)
words	(Old English, before 1000)	*derived*	(French, 1526)
from	(Old English, before 1000)	*different*	(French, 1400)
languages	(Old French, 1290)	*at*	(Old English, before 1000)
different	(French, 1400)	*times*	(Old English, before 1000)

Dividing the words by source language:

Old English (before 1000)

> a, an, any, almost, and, at, come, English, from, find, look, of, one, in, is, the, tells, that, times, up, words, which, where, when, will, you
> (articles, adverbs, conjunctions, prepositions, verbs, nouns, pronouns, adjectives)

Old Norse (by 1200)

> take, they
> (verb, pronoun)

Old French (around 1300)

piece, current, entered, language
(nouns, adjective, verb)

French (*c.* 1400–1500)

derived, different
(verb, adjective)

Latin (1500s)

etymological, dictionary, mixture
(adjective, nouns)

There are 50 words in this passage, some of which are repeated, giving 37 different words. Of these, 27 are Old English, 2 come from Old Norse, 3 from Old French, 2 from French, and 3 from Latin. Note that the dates for these borrowings get steadily later – the Old English words are the oldest, then Old Norse, then Old French, French and Latin.

What we have just done is linguistic palaeontology – searching for fossils (in this case, living ones) in the language. The source languages for these words, and their successive dates of entry, give us a snapshot of the history of the language in Britain.

English came to Britain in the mouths of Germanic people who arrived in the aftermath of the Roman occupation, *c.* 500 AD. As you can see, the majority of the words we use today go back to this period (in the case of this small sample, 73 per cent). About two centuries later, a second wave of invasions and settlements took place, this time from Scandinavia, where people spoke Germanic dialects related to, but distinct from, Old English (these are popularly known as the Viking invasions). To this period we owe a number of very common words (e.g. *take* and *they* in this piece) as well as many dialect words which today survive only in those northern areas of Britain settled by the Scandinavians.

In 1066 England was invaded by speakers of a northern (Viking-influenced) dialect of French, and this became the official language of the country for 300–400 years, bequeathing to us a legacy of Old French derived words (many of which have to do with government and the law – e.g. *court, parliament* as well as *current, entered, language* and *piece*).

Following this, English was re-established as the written language, but borrowings continued from continental French and classical Latin under the influence of the Renaissance (e.g. *derived, different, etymological, dictionary, mixture*). Today, in the absence of physical invasions, English continues to soak up foreign words – *sauna, glasnost, avocado, macho* – as a result of cultural contacts.

Thus we can say that the vocabulary of English is evidence for the history not only of the language, but also of the culture and the people.

But we can go further than this: look at the kinds of words which have come from Old English and Old Norse on the one hand, and Old French, French and Latin on the other. From Old English and Old Norse we get examples of almost every type of word:

articles:	a, an, the	verbs:	come, look, find, take, tell, will
prepositions:	at, of, up, from	nouns:	times, words
conjunctions:	and	adjectives:	English
pronouns:	you, they	adverbs:	almost

but from Old French, French and Latin we get only adjectives, verbs and nouns:

verbs:	enter, derive
nouns:	language, dictionary, mixture, piece
adjectives:	current, etymological, different

In other words, the most frequent words, the words which appear in every text and which work to glue other words together into phrases – words which have a grammatical function – are the oldest. Borrowing seems to occur only into those classes of words which have real-world reference – to things, states, or actions which actually exist (you could, if you wanted to, demonstrate the meaning of *enter* by performing the action, but it would be impossible to demonstrate the meaning of *the* in this way).

Linguistics differentiates between these two types of word: between those which have grammatical function and do not change or get added to, and those which have referential meaning and which do increase in number. It does this by calling one set **closed class** words, and the other **open class**. Above, the closed class ones are on the left, the open on the right.

Stylistics is usually concerned with open class items: this is because the same closed class words are found in all texts, irrespective of subject-matter or level of formality. These items are stylistically neutral: they do not affect the register of a text. Open class words also appear in all texts, but not necessarily the same ones, and they do not all have the same register – for example, compare the Old English/Old Norse verbs *come, look, find, take, tell, will* with the Old French/French/Latin *enter, derive* (and specifically *come in* versus *enter*). Because of the historical associations of Old French with the court and the law, and of French and Latin with learning, words derived from these sources tend to have a higher, that is more formal, register than Old English or Old Norse ones. Thus the open class words often divide between neutral or informal Old English and Old Norse words and more formal Old French, French and Latin ones (e.g. *doggy* and *canine*). Words from French and Latin are also often longer than Old English/Old Norse ones, as recognised by the popular response to overly formal language: 'Don't you use those long words with me!'

In writing, writers can set the stylistic tone or register of their text by consistently selecting either Old English/Old Norse derived words, or Old French, French and Latin derived ones. Much parody or humorous writing relies on deliberately selecting words from an inappropriate source.

Checking derivations

The most authoritative work on the derivation of English words is the *Oxford English Dictionary*, which can be found in most good libraries. This is also now available on CD-ROM – checking large numbers of words is much quicker this way.

Semantics

Examination of a set of 'synonyms' in a thesaurus quickly shows that few words can really be said to 'mean the same thing' – the English lexicon is not a series of paired oppositions between Old English and French or Latin words, but a complex set of relationships between groups consisting of many words. Take, for instance, this list of terms for marked routes:

> alley, lane, street, highway, thoroughfare, road, path, cul-de-sac, avenue, way, ginnel, motorway, expressway, parkway, freeway, boulevard, broadway, main drag, carriageway, bridlepath, back lane, foot path, track, trail

We could analyse the relationship between some of the members of this list in terms of formality (written: *thoroughfare*, *cul-de-sac* versus spoken: *road*, *street*, *path*); it is also possible to see that some words are distinguished according to origin of user (Yorkshire: *ginnel*, Tyneside: *back lane*; UK: *motorway*, USA: *freeway*), frequency of use (current: *motorway*, archaic/rare: *trunk route*), and a whole series of other possible criteria to do with such things as width, length, surface type, surroundings and geography.

Thus, while these terms share a field of meaning (a **semantic field**), it would be simplistic to regard them as 'referring to the same thing'. Rather than thinking of the vocabulary as a set of binary oppositions, it is more useful to consider it as a series of semantic fields – all of which can be structured in terms of formal/informal, current/archaic, technical/non-technical, spoken/written, and so on. To a large extent, the register of a text is determined by a writer consistently selecting words from the same area of different semantic fields.

5.2   Register: use of romance vocabulary

TASK

Using an etymological dictionary, identify the romance vocabulary in Texts 1, 2 and 3 (excluding headings, place names and personal names).
   What is its effect?

TEXT 1

Turnham Green Conservation Area 00248/287/AD1
287 Chiswick High Road, Chiswick, London

Installation of Halo neon lettering to fascia sign of premises and erection of internally illuminated projecting sign.

TEXT 2

Control of Pollution Act 1974
London Borough of Richmond upon Thames
London Borough of Richmond upon Thames (East Twickenham)
Noise Abatement Order 1993

Notice is hereby given that the Council of the London Borough of Richmond upon Thames, in exercise of their powers under Section 63 of the Control of Pollution Act 1974 proposes to make the above Noise Abatement Order. The effect of the order will be to make into a Noise Abatement Zone that part of the London Borough of Richmond upon Thames which is enclosed by the following roads:–
Amyand Park Road, St Margarets Road, Baronsfield Road and Hartington Road.

The Order will apply to the following classes of premises:–
Industrial Premises, Places of Entertainment, Car Repair Workshops and Car Sales Establishments.
When the Order comes into effect the Council is required to register the noise emitted from any premises to which the Order applies. It will be an offence if this registered level is subsequently exceeded without permission of the Council. The council may also, subject to appeal to a Magistrates Court, require the registered level to be reduced.

TEXT 3

When the second war came Shadbold, in his middle thirties, had time to consider the position without undue bustle. He early expressed the conviction, a tenable one, that he would be a liability in the armed forces, and by returning intermittently to schoolmastering, possibly undertaking a short spell of quasi-governmental employment in a rural area towards the close of hostilities, contrived on the whole to steer a course through wartime dangers and inconveniences without undue personal affliction, reducing to a minimum interference with a preferred manner of life. Shadbold never for a moment claimed to have brought off from lofty motive this comparative immunity.

Solution

Romance (e.g. Latin and French) derived words:

TEXT 1

installation, halo, neon, lettering, fascia, sign, premises, erection, internally, illuminated, projecting, sign
(70.5 per cent of the total)

TEXT 2

notice, council, exercise, powers, section, control, pollution, act, proposes, noise, abatement, order, effect, order, noise, abatement, zone, part, enclosed, order, apply, classes, premises, industrial, premises, places, entertainment, repair, establishments, order, effect, council, required, register, noise, emitted, premises, order, applies, offence, registered, level, subsequently, exceeded, permission, council, council, subject, appeal, magistrates, court, require, registered, level, reduced
(40 per cent of the total)

TEXT 3

second, consider, position, undue, expressed, conviction, tenable, liability, forces, returning, intermittently, schoolmastering, possibly, quasi-governmental, employment, rural, area, close, hostilities, contrived, course, dangers, inconveniences, undue, personal, affliction, reducing, minimum, interference, preferred, manner, moment, claimed, motive, comparative, immunity
(36 per cent of the total)

Text 1   London Borough of Hounslow Planning Notice, *Brentford Chiswick and Isleworth Times*, Friday, 3 September 1993, p. 15.

Text 2   London Borough of Richmond upon Thames Notice, *Brentford Chiswick and Isleworth Times*, Friday, 3 September 1993, p. 15.

Text 3   Anthony Powell, O, *How the Wheel Becomes It!*, p. 8.

Verdict

TEXTS 1 AND 2

These short announcements by a local council, in a local newspaper, use a high proportion of Romance-derived vocabulary. Anglo-Norman was the language of the law in England from 1066 until well into the sixteenth century. The law in Britain still requires a high amount of Anglo-Norman French derived vocabulary, and these notices are fulfilling a legal function.

TEXT 3

This text has a high percentage of Romance vocabulary for literature, although not as high as is found in legal texts. This gives the text its learned, pedantic, 'middle-brow literary' style. It is fitting, because the author is demonstrating how Shadbold was claiming to be unsuited to army life, but suited to a teaching one:

> When World War II came Shadbold, in his middle thirties, had time to take stock slowly. He soon said, as was fair enough, that he would not be useful in the army, and by going back every now and then to teaching, maybe doing a bit of hush-hush work in the country at the end of the war, all in all was able to dodge the wartime spills and hiccups without much harm to himself, paring away any messing about with the way he liked things to be. Shadbold never tried to make out he got this fairly safe job in order to do good to others.

If you compare this rewrite with the original, you'll see that what has been lost, among other things, is the 'schoolmastery' tone. This is because the rewrite contains far less Romance vocabulary. The text is now easier to follow, but we lose the feeling that Shadbold is trying to persuade us of the validity of his claim.

5.3   Register: use of 'long' words

What are popularly known as 'long' words, are in fact words which are historically derived from the Classical languages, that is, Ancient Greek and Latin; and also French. They tend to be polysyllabic and learned in register. They can be contrasted with words derived from Germanic languages (usually Old English and Old Norse) which tend to be shorter and more everyday in register (compare *skint* with *impecunious*, or *kill* with *assassinate*).

TEST-FRAME

The best way to find out whether a word is derived from Greek, or Latin or French is to look it up in the *Oxford English Dictionary*, but a good rule of thumb is to check whether it has three or more syllables or is arcane in meaning.

TASK

Without looking anything up, comment on the following text – what is happening?

Do you need to know the meanings of all the words to understand what is going on? Now look up the words you didn't know.

How has this affected the overall effect?

TEXT 4

He began by asking why no action had been taken on his letter. Wagner told him no letter had been received. To make sure of this the Section Head came over to Christie's desk and searched it thoroughly; then he pursued the search on the desks of two other clerks, his secretary, his assistant and his deputy. Try down at Coldharbour Point, thought Christie, with some pleasure, or even Foulness.

Skater's assertive roar when he was told that no letter had arrived could be heard several more desks away; his proposal was that (if he were there) he would defenestrate Wagner. Christie's Section Head was riled at this, and, forgetting he was putting the company's reputation in jeopardy, he suggested that were Skater to come within a hundred yards of him he would (before he could carry out his threat) be subjected to a rapid process of trituration. Skater responded with a distinctly unfair (for it was accurate) divination, from Wagner's telephone manner, of the Section Head's helminthoid resemblances. Wagner snapped back with the only word he could think of at the time, cryptorchid, though as he had never had the necessary opportunity of observing, let alone carrying out a count, Christie felt that his superior had compromised his integrity at this point. And with sounds of gulping incapacitation at both ends of the line the conversation lapsed without any sign of an eirenicon.

Solution

defenestrate: 'to throw out of a window'

triturate: 'to reduce to fine particles or powder by rubbing, bruising, pounding, crushing or grinding'

helminth: 'a worm, especially an intestinal worm'

cryptorchid: 'an individual whose scrotum contains no testicles'

eirenicon: 'a proposal tending to make peace; an attempt to reconcile differences'

ATTRIBUTION

B. S. Johnson, *Christie Malry's Own Double-Entry*, p. 42.

The humour here lies in the incongruity of the Greek and Romance vocabulary in a situation of high emotional temperature, an office argument. At times of high stress and emotion, native English speakers are much more likely to use words of Germanic etymology, as they are the shorter items in the vocabulary and also the more frequently used ones. Hence if we translate the bout of insults into vocabulary of Germanic etymology, we may come up with something like the following:

Skater: If you were here I'd chuck you out the window!
Wagner: If you come within a hundred yards I'll grind you to a pulp first!
Skater: You slimy tapeworm!
Wagner: You bollockless git!

The translation shows that any incongruity lies in the register of the vocabulary, not the meaning.

5.4   Word-formation: bound morphemes

Morphemes are best described as the smallest unit of meaning. Words may consist of one, two, three, or even more morphemes. Each morpheme will add some meaning, for example:

like   (one morpheme)
likely   (two morphemes)
likelihood   (three morphemes)
unlikelihood (four morphemes)

Free morphemes are those which can stand alone; **bound** morphemes have to be added to at least one other morpheme.

unlock	→	*un-* (bound) *lock* (free)
disable	→	*dis-* (bound) *able* (free)
renew	→	*re-* (bound) *new* (free)
agreement	→	*agree* (free) *-ment* (bound)
disagreement	→	*dis-* (bound) *agree* (free) *-ment* (bound)
enclosed	→	*en-* (bound) *close* (free) *-ed* (bound)

Exercises

Identify the bound and free morphemes in the following:

playground

quickly

bathroom

eternally

generally

kindly

completely

forever

somewhere

anything

Comment

playground	→	*play* (free) *ground* (free)
quickly	→	*quick* (free) *-ly* (bound)
bathroom	→	*bath* (free) *room* (free)

eternally	→	*eternal* (free) *-ly* (bound)
generally	→	*general* (free) *-ly* (bound)
kindly	→	*kind* (free) *-ly* (bound)
completely	→	*complete* (free) *-ly* (bound)
forever	→	*for* (free) *ever* (free)
somewhere	→	*some* (free) *where* (free)
anything	→	*any* (free) *thing* (free)

Read the following two texts, noting any unfamiliar words.
How are they constructed? What is their effect?

TEXT 5

Notice was given on 18 June that the Secretary of State for the Environment had called in the planning application made by Thames Water Utilities Ltd to relocate the Perry Oaks sewage sludge dewatering works to Iver South.

TEXT 6

It is hard to believe that there was only one spring and one summer apiece that year, my fifteenth year. It is hard to believe that I so quickly squandered my youth in the sweet town playground of the sunny city, that wild monkeybardom of my fourth-grade youthhood. However, it was so.

'Dear Mother' – I wrote one day on her bathroom mirror with a candle sliver – 'please forgive my absence and my decay and overlook the freckled dignity and pockmarked integrity plaguing me this season.'

I used to come on even wilder sometimes and write her mad cryptic notes on the kitchen sink with charred matches. Anything for a bit, we so seldom saw each other. I even sometimes wrote her a note on paper. And then one day, having romped my soul through the spectrum of sunny colors, I dashed up to her apartment to escape the heat and found a letter from her which eternally elated my heart to the point of bursture and generally endeared her to me forever. Written on the kitchen table in cake frosting was the message, 'My dear, mad, perverse young girl, kindly take care and paint the fire escape in your leisure . . .' All the i's were dotted with marmalade, the t's were crossed with orange rind. Here was a sight to carry with one forever in the back of the screaming eyeballs somewhere. I howled for at least five minutes out of sheer madity and vowed to love her completely. Leisure. As if bare-armed spring ever let up from its invitation to perpetuate the race. And as if we ever owned a fire escape. 'Zweep,' I yelled, not giving a damn for intelligibility and decided that if ever I was to run away from home, I'd take her with me.

Solution

TEXT 5

de-water-ing

TEXT 6

monkey-bar-dom, youth-hood, burst-ure, mad-ity

ATTRIBUTION

Text 5 Department of Environment notice, *Brentford Chiswick and Isleworth Times*, Friday, 3 September 1993, p. 15.
Text 6 Toni Cade Bambara, 'Sweet Town' from *Gorilla, My Love*, pp. 121–2.

It is possible to form new words by adding bound morphemes to already existing words. In each case, the reader will have to deconstruct the new word into its component parts, in order to understand the meaning of the new formation.

TEXT 5

Text 5 shows this process happening in formal, technical language – although we may not know much about the process of sewerage treatment, the purpose of a sludge dewatering works is clear enough!

TEXT 6

Text 6 illustrates the creative, playful aspect of word-formation. Bambara draws on the spoken English of Black Americans in her work, and her use of English has been likened to the playing of jazz musicians. Here, new unfamiliar words are built up with morphemes as a way of illustrating the rich, ebullient imagination of the narrator.

Note that Bambara puts familiar morphemes into unfamiliar pairings to create new words where an ordinary version already exists:

> youthhood – childhood
> bursture – bursting
> madity – madness

The familiarity of the morphemes means that we can understand these words without difficulty, while the freshness of the pairings imparts the frenzied excitement the girl feels as she grows up into a teenager this spring.

5.5 Romance

Identify the Romance vocabulary in Text 7 using an etymological dictionary.
What is its purpose?

TEXT 7 _____

'Even in the wilds of Asia,' Arthur once told me, 'I have never shaved myself when it could possibly be avoided. It's one of those sordid annoying operations which put one in a bad humour for the rest of the day.'

When the barber had gone, Arthur would call to me:

'Come in, dear boy, I'm visible now. Come and talk to me while I powder my nose.'

Seated before the dressing-table in a delicate mauve wrap, Arthur would impart to me the various secrets of his toilet. He was astonishingly fastidious. It was a revelation to me to discover, after all this time, the complex preparations which led up to his every appearance in public. I hadn't dreamed, for example, that he spent ten minutes three times a week in thinning his eyebrows with a pair of pincers. ('Thinning, William; not plucking. That's a piece of effeminacy which I abhor.') A massage-roller occupied another fifteen minutes daily of his valuable time; and then there was a thorough manipulation of his cheeks with face cream (seven or eight minutes) and a little judicious powdering (three or four). Pedicure, of course, was an extra; but Arthur usually spent a few moments rubbing ointment on his toes to avert blisters and corns. Nor did he ever neglect a gargle and mouthwash. ('Coming into daily contact, as I do, with members of the proletariat, I have to defend myself against positive onslaughts of microbes.') All this is not to mention the days on which he actually made up his face. ('I felt I needed a dash of colour this morning; the weather's so depressing.') Or the great fortnightly ablution of his hands and wrists with depilatory lotion. ('I prefer not to be reminded of our kinship with the larger apes.')

Solution

Compare:

> sordid/dirty
> humour/mood
> visible/ready
> impart/tell
> fastidious/fussy

ATTRIBUTION

Christopher Isherwood, *Mr Norris Changes Trains*, pp. 122–3.

Verdict

Romance vocabulary is used in this passage both when there is a less formal (and more expected) alternative (*sordid* vs. *dirty*), and in unusual phrases which don't necessarily have a low-register alternative ('I'm visible now') – this is done in order to show Arthur's fastidiousness. Note how Arthur's camp, highly elaborate style is carried over into the narrative voice ('Arthur would *impart* to me ...') and is not restricted to Albert's direct speech.

The use of Romance vocabulary extends to adjectives (*sordid*, *depilatory*), nouns (*pedicure*, *ablution*, *proletariat*), and verbs (*abhor*). The formal vocabulary is matched by formal pronouns (*one*), relative markers (*which* rather than *that*), formal constructions (*Nor did he ever neglect*) and fastidiously expanded noun phrases (*a thorough manipulation of his cheeks with face cream, members of the proletariat, the larger apes*). This expansion is achieved by the use of premodifiers and adverbs: *possibly, various secrets, astonishingly fastidious, complex preparations, valuable time, thorough manipulation, judicious powdering, positive onslaughts*. The repetition and consistency here give a sense of performance and care which suits Arthur's character. The Romance vocabulary is dressing up the basic process of washing, just as Arthur dresses himself up and removes the hair on his hands and wrists to hide from himself man's base origins.

Indeed, Arthur seeks to remove himself from anything that has connotations of 'manliness' at all, as opposed to 'womanliness'. Arthur may have the body of a man, but he cherishes it in exaggerated female fashion. (Note that the evaluation of this kind of behaviour is totally culture-dependent. For a British man to behave this way in the 1930s was marked as highly aberrant and effeminate; but it is not so interpreted in all cultures, or in all periods.)

5.6 Semantic fields

Definition

Alley, lane, street, highway, thoroughfare, are all part of the *semantic field* of clearings cut to enable people to progress. 'Semantic' is another word for 'meaning'. The previous examples are not synonymous; a lane is usually smaller than a highway, for example; but they cover the same general meaning area, in this case, of roads.

TEST-FRAME

Can two or more words be replaced by one, comprehensive term?

EXAMPLES

I watched the *afghans, scotties, poodles* and *mongrels.*
I watched the *dogs.*

Sometimes a novelist may use several words belonging to the same semantic field. It is always a wordy technique, and if mishandled results in verbosity. Contrast

1   I blocked the alleys, lanes, streets, highways and thoroughfares that led to the hideout.

with

2   I blocked the roads that led to the hideout.

For some readers, (1) will sound more poetic, or will convey the struggle the speaker underwent to block access. For other readers, it will sound tedious and repetitive compared to (2).

TASK

Identify the semantic fields in Texts 8 and 9.

TEXT 8

A shifty unshaven polymath nebbish, with a cocky drone, and a patter so tedious it could have been marketed as a blood-coagulant, was lecturing a dangerously healthy-looking Californian couple. They were shrink-wrapped, sterile, irradiated like a pair of Death Valley grapes. They socked vitamin-enhanced aerobic vitality at you, so hard you could wish on them nothing but a catalogue of all the most repellent diseases of skin and bone and tissue; all the worst back numbers from the cursing books of Ur, Uruk, and Kish. You were obliged to superimpose on their boastful skeletons the historic treasures of old London: growths, malignancies, rickets, nose-warts, furry haemorrhoids, palsies, fevers, sweats, bubos, wens, mouth-fungus, trembles, and pox scabs. They were so heavily insured against disaster that they were almost obliged to justify the premiums by dropping dead before they overdrew another breath.

TEXT 9

With his russet breeches, which descended over his handsome legs into boots so lustrous and pliant I longed to touch and crush them in my hands, he wore a checked and belted red-brown jacket and a maroon silk ascot, and upon his head, a green hat grizzled with silvery veins and proclaiming its continental origin by a *gansbart* sportively stuck in the band. It was no wonder that the old ladies at the Hotel Barstow, too old to be the object of his lascivious eyes, found him charming and said he 'cut a fine figure.' They admired his apparel and said that too often a physician tends to resemble his successor, the mortician. His other suits were of fine materials, all double-breasted and of a cut which did not vary through the years, yet always seemed to be at the peak of fashion. And while the colors and the patterns of the stripes or checks were conservative, the accessory trappings were of the liveliest declensions, being the racing lifeblood of the subdued carcass: neckties (or cravats) of orange silk and crimson wool, printed challis, dotted China silk, pongee, fortified linen, diapered or imprinted with arabesques or stripes or hexagons. His handkerchief and his muffler, if he wore one, matched or complemented the tie as did his socks and the band in his hat. And carrying to its uttermost his nice feeling for detail, he even had alternative spectacles which today, to go with his riding togs, were horn-rimmed, but tomorrow, with blue serge would be rimless octagons, and the next day, if the fancy struck him to dress for dinner and go into Boston, would be a pince-nez with a black ribbon and mother-of-pearl nose-pieces.

TEXT 8

Health	*Insurance*
blood-coagulant	insured
healthy-looking	premiums
sterile	overdrew
irradiated	
vitamin-enhanced	
aerobic	
vitality	
diseases	
skin	
bone	
tissue	
skeletons	
growths	
malignancies	
rickets	
nose-warts	
furry haemorrhoids	
palsies	
fevers	
sweats	
bubos	
wens	
mouth-fungus	
trembles	
pox scabs	

TEXT 9

Clothes; accessories	*Fabric; materials*
breeches	checked
boots	silk
belted	materials

jacket	cut
ascot	stripes
hat, band	checks
apparel	silk
suits	wool
double-breasted	printed challis
accessory trappings	dotted China silk
neckties	pongee
cravats	fortified linen
handkerchief	diapered
muffler	imprinted
tie	arabesques
socks	stripes
band, hat	hexagons
spectacles	serge
riding togs	horn-rimmed
pince-nez	rimless
nose-pieces	ribbon
	mother-of-pearl

ATTRIBUTION

Text 8   Iain Sinclair, *Downriver*, p. 42.
Text 9   Jean Stafford, *Boston Adventure*, pp. 144–5.

Verdict

Both of these texts could have been written much more concisely. In Text 8, the long list of illnesses could have been condensed into the single word *disease*; and in Text 9 the narrator could merely have mentioned that the character described wore fancy clothing.

TEXT 8

In Text 8, the factual content is simply that a salesman is giving his salespitch to a Californian couple. However, the long list of disease terms tells us what the narrator's view of the Californian couple is. This will seem an overly florid rant to some readers, and amusing to others.

TEXT 9

In Text 9 the character described is unreliable, vain and self-centred. The narrator doesn't state this directly. In fact, the narrator is at this point still a child, who has not yet learned to draw inferences from outward appearances and who does not, at this point in the story, know much about the character. However, the reader is able to anticipate something of the character's more unpleasant tendencies by interpreting the numerous terms in the field of clothes as excessive to mere description. The superabundance of terms in this field may intimate a preoccupation with appearance at the expense of moral qualities; but it will depend upon the reader's own views on personal appearance as to whether this inference is drawn or not. A further hint is given, of course, when we are told that the ladies at the hotel are too old 'for his lascivious eyes'.

5.7 Collocation

Definition

Certain words only **collocate** with (that is, appear next to) certain others. Consider the following food terms, all of which contain the meaning, among other things, of becoming unfit for human consumption: *addle, curdle, sour, rancid, stale, fetid*. They collocate with different nouns:

Addle	*Curdle*	*Sour*		*Rancid*	*Stale*	*Fetid*
eggs	milk	milk		bacon	bread	water
brains	cream	cream		butter	cake	gas
		wine			biscuits	
		nature (*of people*)			air	

Words collocate when they occur close together in texts. Some words very frequently collocate – to the extent that they are never found apart – others very rarely occur together. Words can either collocate in set phrases (in which case they will occur close together) or because the introduction of a topic almost inevitably entails the use of the words (in which case they may not be next to each other).

Set phrases trigger strong expectations in readers, which writers can fulfil or disappoint:

baby ____ eyes

(compare *blue* with *green*)

TASK

Read through Text 10, noting the words you expect to find in collocation, and those you don't.

Can you account for the patterns of expected/unexpected collocations?

TEXT 10 ═══

It was a banana echo. And the major suddenly stopped. He dismounted from the camel, took four snakes from his pockets, arranged them carefully on the ground by the tall savanna grasses, placed the camel on them, this tired camel, mounted it again, and then blinked as the snakes carried along gently man and beast in a kayakaya crawl, some roller snakes. To avoid the pricking of pineapple stalks, the snakes had to move carefully, touching the bananas instead, but sometimes forgetting that they were carrying their master and the cheeky camel, for they would suddenly rush after rats and frogs, leaving their master sprawling under the camel. And whenever the snakes apologised in a series of supplicatory wriggles, the major saluted below the camel. Boof, came the salute, shining in the savanna through the reflective gloves that the major wore now. Neems, pines, flamboyants, and frangipani bordered the vast outskirt borders of bananas, pineapples, oranges, and other fruit, crisscrossing the separate areas for carrots.

kayakaya = porter
neem = a large tree

Expected:

> African/tropical collocations:
> *flora*
> banana, savanna grasses, pineapple stalks,
> bananas, neems, pines, flamboyants, frangipani,
> bananas, pineapples, oranges
> *fauna*
> camel, snakes
> *snake collocations*
> crawl, rats, frogs, wriggles
> *military collocations*
> major, saluted, salute, gloves

Unexpected:

> banana – echo
> snakes – carried, roller snakes, forgetting, apologised, supplicatory
> fruit – carrots

ATTRIBUTION

Kojo Laing, *Major Gentl and the Achimota Wars*, p. 90.

Like many pieces of surrealism, this passage works by ensuring that everything is as expected except for one thing. The inclusion of this one feature in a logical way, in an otherwise logical construction, gives the clash of logic and impossibility on which the surreal survives. Here analysis of the collocations shows three main areas which are presented just as they would be in a 'normal' text – the collocations surrounding the African setting and the military theme add up – as do some of the collocations surrounding snakes. But here Laing introduces unexpected collocations – which the reader tries to make sense of because they come in an otherwise 'well-behaved' text. Some readers will find this mere nonsense; others will find the new collocations (for example the wriggling roller snakes) quite delightful.

5.8 Synonyms

Definition

Words which 'mean the same thing' are termed **synonyms** – but in fact few words really do mean exactly the same thing. Words of similar meaning can almost always be distinguished on the basis of their reference and/or register.

In terms of reference, words can be more or less specific, for example:

dog (non-specific) versus *alsatian* (specific)

In terms of register, words can be more or less formal, for example:

mutt → *dog* → *canine quadruped*

TASK

Read Text 11, noting references to the photograph which forms the centre of attention.

Comment on the terms used, and their relationship to each other.

When Biggles, in answer to a call on the intercom, entered the office of his chief, Air Commodore Raymond of the Special Air Section at Scotland Yard, he was greeted with a smile which he knew from experience was not prompted entirely by humour.

'I'm not much for betting, sir, but I'd risk a small wager that what you're going to tell me isn't really funny,' he observed as he pulled up a chair.

'That would depend on how you looked at it,' answered the Air Commodore drily. 'Serious matters can sometimes provoke an ironical smile. Take a look at this. I thought you'd like to see it.' He pushed across the desk a picture that had obviously been cut from a newspaper.

Biggles studied the photographic reproduction for some time without speaking and without a change of expression. It showed a group of seven men standing on a sandy beach with the sea in the background. The subjects were in tropical kit, creased, dirty, shrunken and generally disreputable. They were hatless, and all needed a hair-cut and a shave.

'Recognise anybody?' asked the Air Commodore, whimsically.

'Of course. Our old friend Erich von Stalhein, no less. He appears to have slipped into the soup – on this occasion without being pushed by me.'

'Do you know any of the others?'

'I fancy I've seen one of them before, but not recently, and on the spur of the moment I can't place him. Where, may I ask, was this fascinating snapshot taken?'

'On the coast of north-west Australia.'

Biggles's eyes opened wide. '*Australia*! For Pete's sake! Where will the ubiquitous Erich turn up next? What was he doing there?'

'That's what I'd like to know. At the time the photo was taken he had just come ashore.'

'What did he *say* he was doing?'

'He said he was, or had been, studying oceanography.'

Biggles smiled cynically. 'Imagine von Stalhein sitting on the sea bed watching the winkles and things. How did this enchanting picture come into your hands?'

'It was spotted by Major Charles of Security Intelligence in a batch of newspapers just in from Australia. Actually, the picture was in several papers. He thought we might like to see it.'

Biggles pushed the paper back across the desk. 'You know, sir, von Stalhein is becoming a nuisance.'

Solution

'this', 'it', 'a picture', 'the photographic reproduction', 'It', 'this fascinating snapshot', 'the photo', 'this enchanting picture', 'It', 'the picture', 'it'

ATTRIBUTION

Captain W. E. Johns, *Biggles in Australia*, pp. 5–6.

Verdict

Constant repetition of the same term can become monotonous – so most writers try to vary references to the same item. One way to do this is by pronoun replacement (which we see here with 'this' and 'it'). Another, also employed here, is to use synonyms – though as noted above, few synonyms match perfectly in terms of reference and register, and this method, if pursued too vigorously, can look awkward and contrived.

Here, the list of terms used varies by register and reference. Note how the piece moves from *picture* – which is both non-specific in terms of reference (the term covers many kinds of image apart from photographs) and neutral in terms of register – to 'the photographic reproduction' – much more specific, and formal (because of its Romance derivation). Then, still using specific terms, the piece shifts down the register scale with *snapshot* and *photo* (note that these informal terms occur in speech). It is possible therefore for writers to move along the clines of referential meaning (specificity and formality) independently of each other: an increase in formality does not automatically entail an increase in specificity.

•   •   •

Index

(*Page numbers in italics refer to sections where a term is defined or most fully investigated*)

active voice *49*, 69–71
adjective 4, *5*, 6, 13, 153, 187, 196, 207, 221
adverb (Av) 46, *64–5*, *90–3*, 94–8, 112–16, *120–4*, 149, 191, 207, 221
adverts 3, 13
agent 49, 80, 101
ambiguity 142–7
and 133, 136, 137, 199, 201
article *18–22*, 132, 189, 207
asyndetic coordination *133–9*
auxiliary *do* 192
auxiliary verb (aux) 46, 50, 57, 64–5, 79, 81, 174

Bambara, Toni Cade 86, 97, 218, 219
(to) be 12–13, 27, 69, 77, 101, 189, 192
Beardsley, Peter 65
Beckett, Samuel 178
Bellow, Saul 108
Boehmer, Elleke 100–1
Bond, James 14–15, 91–2
bound morpheme *215–19*
Brentford Chiswick and Isleworth Times 212, 218
Brookner, Anita 10, 11, 160, 161

Burn, Gordon 32, 71

calque *187–95*
Carey, Peter 165
Chandler, Raymond 40, 61–4, 176
chihuahua, a cute little 102, 116
clause *90–3*, 133, 196
closed class vocabulary 207
coherence 124, *164–6*, 176–9, 179–87, 187–95
cohesion 124, *164–6*, 176–9, 179–87, 187–95
collocation 63, *227–30*
complement (C) 10, *90–3*, 94–8, 98, 112–16, 120–1, 145
compound (complex) verb phrase 49, 50, *55–64*, 132
Compton-Burnett, Ivy 175
conjunction 207
Conrad, Joseph 152
coordination 40, *92*, 124–5, 133–9, 164, 199–201

definite article *18*, 132, 137
Deighton, Len 61–4
deixis (deictic terms) *132–3*, 179

235

determiner 2, 5, 189, 196
dialect 37, 41, 195
Dick, Philip K. 189
Doyle, Roddy 178
dummy subjects 189

ellipsis 106, 164, *170–6*, 179
enumerator 2, 196
exclusive pronoun 29 ˙

Faulkner, William 112, 142
finite verb phrase *46–9*, *55–6*, 64, 80,
    82, 83–8
Fitzgerald, F. Scott 25, 28–9, 152
Fitzgerald, Zelda 131
Fleming, Ian 16
free morpheme 215–19
French 204–9, 213

genre 166
Gibbons, Stella 37
Greek 213
Green, Henry 25, 26, 29, 115, 131, 198
Greene, Graham 123

Hall, Adam 61–4, 137, 138
head noun 2, 93, 145, 187
Healy, Thomas 122
heaviness (syntactic weight) 92, *100–1*,
    102, 113, 116
Helsinki 58, 65

I 27
idiolect 23, 176
Ijaw 191
imperative *72–6*
inclusive pronoun 29
indefinite article *18*
infinitive *77–80*
information (given and new) *91–2*, 113,
    124, *166–70*
-*ing* form *80–3*, 87
intercalated clause *196–8*
interrogative *156–61*
intransitive *109–12*, 145
Isherwood, Christopher 82, 221

James, Henry 119, 142
Japanese 189
Johns, Captain W. E. 232
Johnson, B. S. 214
Joyce, James 185

Kipling, Rudyard 54, *55*

Laing, Kojo 229
Latin 204–9, 213
Lodge, David 54, *55*

main clause 93, *124–33*, 141
main verb 46, *94*, 120
Masters, John 32
Mathews, Harry 75
Maugham, Somerset 10
McInerney, Jay 108
Mo, Timothy 160, 161
modal verb 57
morphology 49–50, 64, *215–19*
Mukherjee, Bharati 37

Nabokov, Vladimir 21, 98
Naipaul, Shiva 79
Naipaul, V. S. 136
narrator 10–11, 12, 21, 27, 29, 54,
    62–3, 71, 79, 83, 102, 112, 143,
    147, 155, 161
negative particle 46
News of the World 13
newspaper English 4, 13
non-finite verb phrase 47, *55–6*, 63–4,
    77–80, *80–3*, *83–8*
Norman French 187
noun phrase (NP) 2–5, *5–44*, 72, 90–3,
    94, 98–102, 115, 133, 136, 143,
    149, 152, 170, 196, 207, 222, 227
number 5, 46–7, 98

object (O) 5, 10, 22, *90–3*, *94–8*, 98,
    112–16, 120–1
Okara, Gabriel 191, 193
Old English 204–9, 213
Old French 187, 204–9
Old Norse 204–9, 213
one 22–3, 27, 34
open class vocabulary *207*
oral storytelling 194
Orwell, George 25, 27–8, 29
Oxford English Dictionary 208, 213

passive voice *49*, *69–71*, 77
past participle *80–1*, 87
past tense 48–90, 54, 132
person 5, 46–7, 79, 83–8, 98
possessive pronouns 4, 22
postmodification 2, *12–17*, 115, 187
Powell, Anthony 212
premodification 2, *5–12*, 221
prepositional phrase (PP) 132, 143,
    147–55, 207

present tense 48–9, *54*, *64–7*, 79, 101
pronoun 2, *4–5*, *22–9*, *29–34*, *34–44*,
    72, 102, 116, 125, 164, 179, 196,
    207, 221, 232

register 2098–12, 213–15, 232
relative clause 145, *199–201*, 221
Rhys, Jean 67
Richardson, Dorothy 185
romance vocabulary 209–12, 220–2

Samsom, William 79
scientific English 69
Selvon, Sam 42–3
semantic field *208–9*, 222–7
sentence *93*, 140–2
sex and shopping novel 17
simple verb phrase 49, *55–64*, 87, 132,
    194
Sinclair, Iain 226
sludge dewatering works 219
Smith, Stevie 201
spoken English 2, 10, 13, 72, 113, 115,
    165, 166, 170, 174, 175, 176,
    195–201
Stafford, Jean 32, 226
subject (S) 5, 46–7, 49, 71, 77, 80–1,
    90–3, *94–8*, 98–102, 102–9, 115,
    116–20, 145, 166–7, 174
subordinate clause *93*, 121, 124–33,
    140–2, 145
subordinate verb 120
subordination *92–3*, 109, 115, 124–33,
    134, 140–2, 164, 199–201
SVX structure 97–8, 99–101, *102–9*,

109–12, 112–16, 116–20, 120–4,
    164, 192
Swift, Graham 21, 166
syndetic coordination *133–9*
synonym 208–9, 222, 230–3
syntax (clause structure) *90–3*, *94–8*

tense 46–7, *48–9*, *49–55*, 64–7, 79,
    80–1, 83–8
text structure *164–6*
trade names 17
transitive *109–12*, 145
Trinidadian English 42–3
Tutuola, Amos 193

verb phrase 2, 10, 46–9, 49–88, *90–3*,
    98–102, 102–9, 109–12, 143, 148,
    149, 176, 207, 221
vocabulary *204–9*, 209–33
voice 47–8, *69–71*

Wain, John 174, 175, 176
Wallington, Mark 169
Watt, Ian 120
we 22–3, *29–34*
Wells, H. G. 145
word-formation *215–19*
written English 10, 72, 139, 165, 170,
    195–201
X element *90–3*, *94–8*, 98–102, 102–9,
    112–16, 116–20, 120–4, 141, 166–7

Yoruba 193
you 23, *34–44*